Chase One Rabbit:

10 Habits that Move You from Failure to Success

Dr. Philip Kim

three boys press

10/2/14

To Kelly:

To my friend & colleague ~ thank you for your support & encouragement!

-Phil Kim

Chase One Rabbit:
10 Habits that Move You from Failure to Success

Published by:
Three Boys Press, a subsidiary of Ideapath Consulting, LLC, Canal Fulton, Ohio.

First Edition

Printed in the United States of America

For book ordering or permission requests, write or email the publisher, at the address below:

Ideapath Consulting, LLC
9751 Diamond Ridge Circle
Canal Fulton, OH 44614
www.ideapathconsulting.com

Praise for *Chase One Rabbit: 10 Habits That Move You From Failure To Success...*

"This enjoyable, practical book gives you a series of simple techniques you can use today to get complete control of your time and your life."

■ **Brian Tracy**
Best Selling Author of *Time Power*

"You won't be able to put this book down! No matter what change you want to make in your life, these words will empower you to begin today and stick with it. Not only are the principles incredibly powerful...Phil uses illustrations that engage your heart as well as your mind! Life-changing!"

■ **Glenna Salsbury, CSP, CPAE**
Author of *The Art of The Fresh Start*

"*Chase One Rabbit* is an excellent reminder of the importance of setting realistic short term goals to achieve long term success."

■ **Todd Brice**
CEO and President of S&T Bank

"In his delightful book, *Chase One Rabbit*, Philip Kim helps you get clarity and focus on the most important, bite-sized things you can and should do to create your own success. Phil has a wonderful way of telling stories that makes his principles for productivity come alive with meaning for anyone."

■ **Joe Calloway, CSP, CPAE**
Author of *Be the Best At What Matters Most*

"I dare you to open to any page in this book and not find something inspirational or educational. You can't "hang out" with Phil's Rabbit Habits without getting a serious boost to higher success."

■ **Kordell Norton, CSP**
Speaker, Consultant, Trainer
Author of *Throwing Gas on the Fire*

"This is a remarkable book about perseverance, finding a way to give yourself a second chance, and the strategies necessary for success. It should be required reading for college students, entrepreneurs, and anyone who wants to achieve more success. I myself will refer to it often."

■ Maribeth Kuzmeski
President of RedZone Marketing
Author of 7 books including *The Connectors*

"How do you move from repeated failure to success? In his book, Phil shares his stories and insights that are sure to intrigue and inspire you to look beyond your failures and develop your own success habits."

■ Jon Petz, CSP
Author of *Boring Meetings Suck*

"This is an excellent book! It is filled to the brim with practical and insightful tips that anyone could use to be more productive."

■ Dr. Cory Maloney
Professor of Business at Franciscan University

"By providing an open window to his past and describing how his struggles led to success, Dr. Kim's message becomes relatable to the reader. *Chase One Rabbit* is a must read for anyone that wants to squeeze the most productivity out of their existing skills and experiences."

■ Brian J Kolowitz, DSc., MSc., MBA
Principal Healthcare Information Systems Architect

"Everyone goes through failure, it's how you respond to life's setbacks that determines your success. *Chase One Rabbit* will help you do that, one step at a time. Start reading this book today!"

■ Lisa Ryan
Chief Appreciation Strategist, Best-Selling Author, and
Internationally Recognized Gratitude Expert

Dedication

To my wife Amanda.
I väve.

And to our precious boys
Be good.

To my dad – who won't read this book until
it's translated into Korean.

To everyone who has failed in life and feels like giving up.

Keep going. It's not over yet.

Table of Contents:

Introduction: Growing Up Korean

Growing up I knew I was different. Before I said a word, I was an outsider.

My parents emigrated from South Korea to the US in the late 60s. My sister and I were born in the States, but English was my second language. At home we spoke Korean; we ate Korean food, and celebrated Korean holidays, culture, and rituals. I remember hating it. I just wanted to be like all the other kids at school. I didn't want kimchi; I wanted pizza. Forget chopsticks; American kids use forks. I had the classic Asian bowl cut and high pants. I can recall names like chink and slanty-eyes. Kids can be cruel sometimes. I was born and raised in Philadelphia, PA but people still asked, "No, where are you *really* from?" All I wanted was to fit in.

Failing

Every year more than 3 million students fail to graduate from high school. Those who come from the lower quartile of family income are seven times more likely to drop out of high school. The statistics are even worse for black (10%) and Hispanic (18%) students. [1]

Are you in this category of failure? I am. I am a high school dropout. Contrary to common stereotypes, I am Korean, play piano, and wear thick glasses and I <u>still</u> didn't do well in school. For middle class Asians growing up in mostly white neighborhoods, the high school dropout rate is almost negligible at 2%.

The irony is, as a full-time college professor, most if not all of my students have achieved something that I have not. Most of them have their high school diplomas. The sheer and utter unlikelihood of my failure made me a classic example of *what not to do.*

In the early summer of 1995, while the rest of my senior class was walking up the auditorium stage to receive their diplomas, I was sitting at home watching TV. I was a mass of self-pity. This was not supposed to be me.

I was an outlier for all the wrong reasons. The deck was totally stacked in my favor and yet, according to my father, I had now became a story of woe for the entire nation of South Korea. At the time, the hardest thing about dropping out of high school was the shame of what it would do to my dad and his reputation within the Korean business community.

I can't quite confirm this yet, but believe I may have been the only high school dropout in the entire history of Korean immigrants. Of the hundreds of family members and friends that came over to the States and didn't know how to speak English, they all at least graduated high school. I truly was a national disgrace.

As the realization of my abject failure set in, my father decided we needed to talk. *This was it, he was going to do the merciful thing and kill me.* My life was over anyway, he was only doing what a Korean father should do.

Then the unexpected happened. He extended grace. He told me he loved me no matter what choices I've made.

Then he said it was time to grow up. I was an adult now and, at the ripe age of 18, I was going to be on my own. He told me I had some difficult choices ahead of me, but they were mine to make. I had no clue what I was going to do, but was grateful for another chance.

It's not over until you quit.

The beauty of desperation is you can't close off any possible opportunities. I was anxious to move on from my high school debacle. I wanted to do something more with my life. I was desperate to be more than a statistic.

By some miracle, my guidance counselor encouraged me to not give up on college. He suggested pursuing a General Equivalency Diploma (GED). Remember, this was before Google so I had no clue what a GED was. I thought the road to my future was completely closed off, but here was *another way to get to where I wanted to go*.

> **"Human beings are the only creatures who are allowed to fail. If an ant fails, it's dead. But we're allowed to learn from our mistakes and from our failures. And that's how I learn, by falling flat on my face and picking myself up and starting all over again." ~ Madeleine L'Engle**

You can't constantly live in regret. You've made mistakes. Learn from them, but don't dwell on them. Successful people have amazingly short memories.

No matter how careful and well thought out your plans are, sometimes they just don't work. You miss things. Your kids get sick. You're still stuck at the same dead-end job. You get thrown a curveball when you're expecting a fastball. You get frustrated because your dreams and goals have not come out the way you planned.

It's times like these when we need a serious reboot.

Our brains are like smartphone operating systems. They control the way we think, process, and download information. Have you noticed sometimes that your super-duper-phone gets bogged down? The trusty apps start to crash, there are too many open programs, and you're loaded with tons of adware and bloatware.

It's time to shut it down and restart the old O/S. You may even have to uninstall some old apps you don't use anymore.

Your life is no different. You know something's not working, but you don't know what to do. Out of nowhere the old way of doing things doesn't apply now. You will have to delete some old habits and re-focus your efforts to develop new habits that play to your strengths.

There's a quote by Confucius that captures this essence: **"Chasing both rabbits leads to catching neither."**

Chase One Rabbit is a book about the power of focus and achieving small wins. My goal is to help you move from past your failures and focusing on small and measurable steps towards attaining your goals.

Success is a Choice

When I am counseling and advising young and seasoned professionals, the hardest thing to grasp is that they can still be successful after failure. It's a simple but profound truth.

Twenty years later, I still remember that life-changing moment with my dad. Success is a choice. You are the only one who can make this choice. The old way of doing things just doesn't work anymore – you need to redefine your approach.

> **It takes a lot more perseverance and courage to finish something than it does to start something.**

It doesn't matter where you are in life. Even if you are a 'complete failure' with no job and no prospects, it's not too late for you. You're not too old, too poor, too uneducated, too fat, too thin, too whatever. You have a choice. You can continue on the path that got you nowhere, or you can choose a new one.

I hope as you read this book you will be inspired to act. Some of the techniques and tips you read may not be new. That's okay. It's like losing weight or starting a new exercise regimen. We know what we ought to do, but don't actually do it. Sometimes we start, but give up too soon before we see results. Stop jumping from one idea to the next.

You're chasing too many rabbits. Start with one.

Introduction Notes:

1.   http://www.statisticbrain.com/high-school-dropout-statistics/

"Success is a result of small efforts day in and day out."

~ Robert Collier

Chapter 1: The Power of Small Wins

The First 7 Minutes

I have a friend who's a runner. He runs 5 times a week, enters races, and talks about his times. You know the type. Every person has a friend like this. I am not a runner. I've never been one and I don't plan on being one. You're either born with that "I love to wear neon shorts and go running" gene or you're not. And I am most definitely not.

I asked him how his training regimen was progressing. He runs three half-marathons a year, and this is the year he's going to try for his personal best of running 13.1 miles in under two hours. Can you imagine running for over two hours straight? *What planet are these people from?* Maybe you're a runner and this is normal. While this may not seem like blazing speed to you, keep in mind he's 56 years old. Here's the real kicker, he started running when he was 50.

He's only been running for 6 years. And the first time he ran, he couldn't. He had to stop after three minutes. He said he barely made it three blocks from his house when he realized he didn't want to die in front of his neighbors. He stopped and turned back home.

The next week he gave it another shot. Surprisingly, he made it past the three blocks and he could continue walking. The week after that he got up to seven minutes straight jogging without walking. He knew he looked ridiculous running this slow, but he stuck to a pace he could handle. He found that seven minutes was a magic number because he couldn't see his house anymore. No turning back now. The seven minutes soon became 15 minutes, which progressed to 30 minutes and so on.

Here's the thing, he still hates running.

He knows fellow runners who claim to enjoy it, but you don't have to love something to do it. It's good for his heart and that's enough motivation to get him past the first 7 minutes. He still contends even now, after 6 years and multiple 10K and half marathon races, that the first 7 minutes are the hardest. Once you get past that first mile, it becomes easier. You may not be able to run 13.1 miles today in under 2 hours, but you can certainly start with 7 minutes.

Small Steps

We should all have big dreams and visions of our future lives. But if you simply hold onto your dreams without any doable action steps, they remain dreams. So what is your dream? What immediately comes to mind when you think of your dreams?

It could be your first book, a big promotion, or starting your very first business. It could be all three. What are the dreams and big ideas that capture your imagination?

Contrary to what others say about always keeping your eye on the prize, if you only focus on the end goal, you can become easily discouraged. Can you remember the last time you were inspired to get healthier and lose those extra pounds? You finally saw yourself on Facebook or Instagram without a filter. *Yes, that is what you really look like.* (Time to untag and unfriend some people.) Then what happens? You become fired up. Nothing is going to stop you this time. You go out and purchase the latest fruit juicer Vitamixer 3000 machine, sign up for 2 years' worth of P-90-million-X, and buy bright orange runner's shoes. Alas, your glorious body awaits you.

You know what happens. Two weeks later, the juicer and P-90-gazillion-X DVDs collect dust or we sell it for 90% discount on Craigslist. I propose that all diet-related products should have a 24 month full return policy. No questions asked. This gives us just enough time to regain our sanity. The depreciation on these things is worse than a used Kia.

People often get discouraged when they don't see immediate results.

It's like watching your own child grow up. You don't notice it nearly as much as the grandparents do, because you see them every day. The small incremental changes are critical to proper growth, but the big milestones get all the attention. Don't get too caught up in the big changes. They only happen because of the consistency of small changes.

Don't Make Up for Lost Time

Don't try to do everything in one day. There is something in us that wants to make up for lost time and we immediately go overboard.

Don't try to make up for lost time. It's like opportunity cost. Once that time has passed, it's gone. There is no recouping those losses. Don't double down on lost time. The best thing to do is move forward with the opportunities you have in front of you.

The quality of what you're working on will suffer if you try to cram everything into one sitting. It's like my students who try to cram 8 chapters into one caffeinated 'study' fest only to find themselves exhausted, unprepared, and not ready for exam day.

It doesn't work.

Chunking

What does work is chunking. Take your dream and break it down into small, doable chunks. Work on the first small step. Complete it. Then work on the next.

Concentrate on doing a great job on the small action chunks.

Want to hear my dreams turned into small doable action chunks?

Goal #1: Finish this book.

Action Chunk #1: Write for 15 minutes every day.

Yes, this means finding 15 minutes to complete my writing. But isn't my writing, business, and dream worth the extra 15 minutes? This is how I was able to finish over 20 published articles, my first e-book, and continue to post on my blog regularly at: http://write15minutes.com.

Is your personal goal worth an extra 15 minutes of your time? If it's not, then you don't have a big enough dream.

Goal #2: Lose 20 lbs.

Action Chunk #1: Start with 10 push-ups a day for a week.

I, along with over 70% of Americans, can bear to lose a few pounds. Ahem, okay a lot of pounds. I'm doing what's called the 100 Push-Up Challenge. That's right, there's actually a website, book, and exercise program based on the pushup. The evil pushup. I hate them, but I know they're good for me. This program starts you off at the beginner stage. You start small. There's no way I can do 100 pushups, but I'm getting there with small, simple steps.

The simplicity is in the small chunks. Here's what I mean.
- Set #1: 2 pushups (rest 60 seconds)
- Set #2: 3 pushups (rest 60 seconds)
- Set #3: 2 pushups (rest 60 seconds)
- Set #4: 2 pushups (rest 60 seconds)
- Set #5: max (at least 3 pushups)

By the end of the set, at minimum I've done 12 pushups for the day. Now who can't do a set of 3 pushups at a time? And by the end of 6 weeks, I will have worked up to 100 total pushups.

But it begins with the first step. 12 pushups done. In less than 5 minutes. Boom.

Time for a donut.

So what are those dreams that you can break down into smaller, doable action chunks?

"Don't let the fear of time it will take to accomplish something stand in the way of your doing it. The time will pass anyway; we might just as well put that passing time to the best possible use." ~ Earl Nightingale.

Don't worry if your dream takes time.

Things that are worth pursuing often take time to develop. Overnight successes are a myth. What you don't see in the background is years of hard work, failure, rejection, devotion, and a committed focus to making a dream come true.

Roxanne Quimby, co-founder of Burt's Bees, was a single mother living with her two kids and no electricity.

While waiting tables at the age of 36, she became an entrepreneur by selling local honey provided by Burt Shavitz, her beekeeper boyfriend. As honey sales grew, Roxanne knew she could sell peripheral products like beeswax candles. This led to further products like beeswax furniture polish, moisturizer, and lip balm.

Early on, Roxanne had to make difficult decisions, like relocating from Maine to North Carolina because there were legal complications with hiring practices and labor laws. She knew that, in order to grow the business, Burt's Bees would have to be ruthless in making hiring and product cuts. Sometimes products that once sold well became clunkers. When some products didn't work she wasn't emotionally attached to them. Roxanne was thinking for the long haul and not just the short term gains.

On a personal note, both my boys have had serious allergic reactions to all brands of sunscreen, except for Burt's Bees Sunscreen. I am grateful that Roxanne didn't stop innovating and improving her business when she had achieved a moderate level of success.

> **Success doesn't come from one brilliant idea, but from a bunch of small decisions.**

Angry Birds

If you have an iPhone, you are probably familiar with Angry Birds. It's become so ubiquitous in its merchandising you've most likely seen Angry Birds t-shirts, the board game, key chains, and shot glasses. There's even Angry Birds toilet paper. Not quite sure how this promotes the brand, but they have it now.

What you don't see are the *50+ other games they developed before* Angry Birds that didn't make the cut. Rovio, the company that developed Angry Birds game was on the brink of bankruptcy and had decided this last game would be the make or break business plan for them. Today, the Angry Birds brand is said to be valued at over $1B (that's with a B). It took over 50 iterations to get there, but the smash hit wouldn't have been possible without the earlier small steps.

WD-39

Dr. Norm Larsen, a real rocket scientist, was concerned about the effect of water corrosion and rust on rockets and nuclear missiles. Larsen's target market was the aerospace industry and his invention was Water Displacement #40, now widely known as WD-40. It took 39 failures and, finally, on the 40th attempt, the formula was complete. Even after proving the concept to space engineers, it still took five additional years to get the product to the consumer market.

It's one of the most widely used solvents in the world with uses ranging from loosening a squeaky door hinge to removing paint and crayon marks from walls. According to the WD-40 website there are over 2000 uses for it.

Even crazier, a bus driver in Asia used WD-40 to remove a python, which had coiled itself around the undercarriage of his bus. In another story, Police Officers reportedly used WD-40 to remove a naked burglar trapped in an air conditioning vent.

Imagine if Larsen had given up after try #39? The python would still be riding the bus and the air conditioning would still not work.

Don't look at failures as unfortunate missteps. Look at them as small strides towards getting you closer to your goal.

"Don't be afraid to give your best to what seemingly are small jobs. Every time you conquer one it makes you that much

stronger. **If you do the little jobs well, the big ones tend to take care of themselves." ~ Dale Carnegie**

I love this diagram from Sarah Lou Davies (@WorkExperiment) at http://www.theworkexperiment.com:

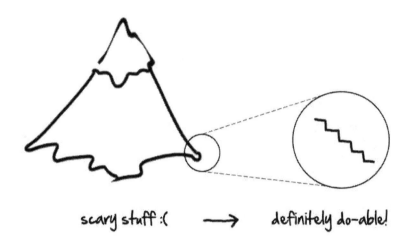

scary stuff :(⟶   definitely do-able!

think big, start small
© The Work Experiment 2011
sarah.theworkexperiment.com

"When I face the desolate impossibility of writing five hundred pages, a sick sense of failure falls on me, and I know I can never do it. Then gradually, I write one page and then another. One day's work is all I can permit myself to contemplate."

~ John Steinbeck, *Travels with Charley: In Search of America*

A series of small wins = Great results

Don't sweat starting small. Sometimes it's the only way to get started.

Don't Force It

Be yourself. If some of the things work for you, that's great. But you may have to alter and change some of the ideas here to better fit your personality. You may not be in a position of leadership right now and some concepts and techniques may have to wait on the backburner until you are in a position of influence.

Often I read other authors and listen to speakers and I think I wish I could write like Malcolm Gladwell or be as funny as Jerry Seinfeld, but that's not me. I have my own writing style and wicked sense of humor. If I try to write or speak like them, it will look awkward and forced. Don't do it. Find something that you really love and doesn't feel forced.

> **Perseverance is not a long race; it is many short races one after another.**
> **~ Walter Elliott**

Pay attention to the small details. Meaningful events and critical turning points will only be recognized if you are actually looking for them.

The path to achieving more is open to everyone. It requires a strong desire to learn new methods and techniques but also a commitment to apply them. Break down your big dreams into small goals.

The 1% Rule

For retirement professionals, there is a well-known number: 72. The rule of 72 relates to the amount of time it takes for your investment to increase by 100%. So if your rate of return is 12%, it will take approximately 6 years for your investment to double.

The same is true with our own personal development. If you were to improve yourself by 1% each day in a little over 2 months you would be 100% better. That's the magic of compounding, known as the 1% rule. Every little bit helps. Even a tiny improvement over time can have a dramatic impact on your personal productivity and success.

Chapter 1 Notes:

1. Sara Lou Davies. (2013). The Work Experiment. Retrieved from http://theworkexperiment.com.

> **"I am not concerned that you have fallen -- I am concerned that you arise."**
>
> **~ Abraham Lincoln**

Chapter 2: Forget Yesterday

You know what's so great about yesterday? It's over. You can't go back. Stop reliving those mistakes. You can't go back and change the way you did things, because yesterday is gone. And tomorrow won't get here until, well, tomorrow. But today is here right now.

Perhaps you've made some choices that you wish you could take back. I get that. We all do. But it's what steps you take now that matter. For most of us, we can't completely forget the past, because it is who we are and it has influenced us today, but don't let that define you.

Leonardo da Vinci ... the Accountant?

In 1452, in a tiny village of Vinci (near Florence, Italy), Leonardo was born to a poor peasant woman named Caterina. His father, Ser Peiro da Vinci, a very prosperous accountant and notary, was not married to Caterina, and thus disqualified Leonardo from following in the footsteps of his father's business. His family was able to send him to apprentice under Andrea del Verrocchio, a master painter and sculptor.

He apprenticed under Verrocchio for 6 years before he was able to advance. Read that again. Leonardo spent 6 years cleaning the shop, doing mundane tasks, and being an apprentice while he worked on his craft.

He didn't have a choice in what family he was born into. Our background, family, and medical history have little to do with our decisions. It's something we're born with or have little to no control over.

It's what you do with what you can control that determines your destiny.

What would have happened if his rich father married his poor mother?

We probably would have only known Leonardo da Vinci as the amazing accountant. Certainly a noble profession, but we wouldn't have the Mona Lisa, the Last Supper, or the Vitruvian Man (look it up, you'll recognize it).

What would have happened if Leonardo da Vinci decided he'd had enough after 1, 2, or even 5 years? Don't quit too soon, the next breakthrough you need could be just around the corner.

I Was an Early Criminal

I remember the first time I broke the law. I was still living with my parents at the time. To this day, I still can't believe I got away with it. I knew my window of opportunity was small, and I had to strike fast. I crept into my parents' room, found the change jar, carefully pulling out precious 50 cent coins one by one. For those who don't know what 50 cent coins look like, they are over twice the size of quarters and have some weight to them. They felt like thick gold medallions to my juvenile-delinquent, 6-year-old hands.

I fashioned a home-made pouch out of notebook paper and Scotch tape. I must have had over $40 in total. There were some dollar bills in the jar, I took those too. I had it all planned out.

The night before my escape, I placed my bike at the end of our long driveway, so my parents couldn't see it. I could barely get to sleep that night, I was so anxious. The next morning, while I should have been walking to the bus stop, I hopped on my bike and started racing down the other way. There was no time to lose. My parents would soon be driving this route to work, and I knew that, if I rode as fast as I could, I would be able to make it to the K-Mart store, a mere 3 miles away.

I flew. In my mind I envisioned my mom jumping into her minivan in her bathrobe, tracking me down like a rogue CIA agent. I was doing it. I was actually skipping school. I was only in first grade, and I knew this was breaking the law, but nothing was going to hold me back.

Then I heard the sickening 'clink-clink' sound that coins make when they're falling on pavement. My makeshift paper purse was leaking. All that money and weeks of planning were slipping out of my pockets. I was leaving a shiny money trail as I sped along the busy road. I screeched to a stop. How could this happen? I envisioned my parents appearing out of thin air and dragging me back home to lock me up for life. I knew I had to make a decision. I estimated a loss of about 15 - 20 coins. I had to take care of what precious coins I had left. Like fallen soldiers, the dropped coins were dead to me now. I leapt back onto my bike and begged for speed.

My eyes burned as I fought back tears. I feared that, if I didn't get to the K-Mart fast, I would lose even more money and the entire day would be a waste. I finally made it down the main stretch of road. Just a couple more blocks. And then I saw her. I didn't see her per se, but I saw the light blue van. It was her van. Mom was going to work and coming down the same exact stretch of road. Horrified, my burning legs found new energy and pumped even faster. I couldn't look back. *Clink. Clink. Clink.* More perished coins. Those blasted coins. I don't know what was worse, being caught by my mom or losing all that money.

As she was about to overtake me, I quickly turned my head away to avoid eye contact, but as I turned my head, I found myself staring directly into a clock repair shop. The plate glass window storefront provided a perfect reflection of me and my mother side by side in slow motion as if we were posing for some bizarre family photo.

I saw her face. I slowed down and pulled over. This was it. *I'm dead.*

I shut my eyes and waited. I wasn't going to cry. That's for babies. I waited a little more and nothing happened. No screeching of tires, honking, or yelling of Korean obscenities in my direction.

Wait, had she actually seen me? Even if she had, how could she possible know it was me?

It could have easily been any other chubby Asian boy wearing a Catholic school uniform riding her son's bike. I froze. I couldn't move for what seemed like an eternity.

Still nothing. *Free at last.*

I tried to go the rest of the way to K-Mart, but my legs were too shaky. I sat down in the blazing sun. This whole fiasco took place in a span of two minutes, but it felt like I had been riding for days. I took out my *Masters of the Universe* lunch box and drained my Capri Sun and ate my pork dumplings.

I knew I had at least another mile to go before reaching the K-mart, but I wasn't sure if I'd make it. And if my mom was going to look for me, she would go there first. I loved K-mart. G.I. Joe action figures and arcade games can make kids do stupid things. Change of plans. I turned into the first shopping plaza I saw on the main strip and went to the furthest store in the lot, an Acme Food Store.

No way would she look here. I had only been in this Acme store once or twice before. This was where old people shopped; no kids' toys here. I was hoping they had at least one arcade game machine.

As if the heavens parted, I could see Ms. Pac-Man and Galaga standing side by side, my two favorites! It's been said the view from the mountain is always worth it when you've made it to the top. I'm here to tell you it's true, my friends.

I wasted no time. I ran to the game console and pulled out my tattered paper purse. I knew I still had over $10 left in my wallet. This was going to be a great day after all. It was only then I realized these machines **only take quarters**.

All of the careful thought and planning I put into this day unraveled because I didn't think of the most basic thing. In order to play video games, you need quarters. I was heartbroken.

In retrospect, I probably could have figured out a way to get my money exchanged for quarters, but I hit a certain point where I wasn't going to try anymore. I gave up. I didn't have it in me to be the charming 1st grader I normally was. I reached my limit. I bought an Archie and Jughead comic book, a hot dog, and trudged home.

I'm not advocating juvenile truancy. That's against the law in this country.

What I am advocating is letting go of past failure. As I said, I am a high school dropout. As you can see, I had absolutely no interest in formal education. Even at the ripe age of six, I knew the utter joy and freedom of cutting classes. Ironically enough, this is my profession now.

I teach and train college students, adult learners, and executives on various topics and productivity improvements. If one were to look at my track record throughout grade school all the way up to my 5+ years in pursuing my undergraduate degree, I was clearly not the best student. Some would say I had a complete disregard for the tenets of education like 'showing up to class,' 'paying attention,' and 'taking exams' – you know, all the ridiculous stuff teachers like to require in order for their students to pass.

I'd love to reach out to my former grade school teachers and ask them if they remember me. If they do, it is probably only as a trouble-maker or permanent resident in detention hall.

My past could not have predicted my future.

My past did not impact my future.

What is in your past that limits your view of your future dreams? Stop sabotaging your dreams with self-limiting beliefs.

Negativity Bias

Did you know that we are drawn to negativity? Without prompting, people are more likely to remember negative aspects of their lives. This has been researched by social scientists and they have a name for it. It's called the *negativity bias*.

According to a report by the *Harvard Business Review*[1], when asked to recall emotional events, respondents reported four negative memories to everyone. You are 80% more likely to recall a negative memory than a positive one.

Isn't this absurd? With the majority of positive occurrences in our lives, our brains naturally gravitate towards the negative bias.

Have you ever had a performance review conducted by your supervisor? Can you remember how this felt? For most of us, we can listen to 25 minutes of nothing but glowing praise, but guess what we remember? The one or two minutes that can be described as areas of improvement or deficiencies.

The human paradox is people remember criticism but respond to praise.[2]

What Matters is How You See It

How do you view failure? Do you look at failing as an opportunity to grow? Do you see it as a chance to learn, adapt, and change?

This is one of the most fundamental elements to success in your life.

Ask yourself: How do I view failure?

Consider your past letdowns and how you've responded to past failures.

If there is a wall that blocks your path, is your first response to give up and go home or do you look to find an alternative route to your destination?

Failure is Not Final

Failing is often one the best ways we figure new things out.

Think of failing as allowing yourself to try new things and experiment and expand your boundaries. Failing fast is even better because you learn more quickly. Ultimately you only become a failure if you stop trying.

Recently, I was listening to a presentation at Carnegie Mellon University, where speaker and author Scott Berkun was discussing the idea of innovation and creativity. During his talk, Scott referred to 3M – a century old company which prospers on innovation. Everyone has either heard of or used one of 3M's products from Post-It Notes to Scotchgard and Scotch tape.

One of the key leaders in 3M's history was William McKnight, who led the company from the brink of bankruptcy to its largest growth period from 1929 to 1966. Even more than the vast array of products, 3M was known for its management culture that emphasized employee independence, delegation of responsibility, and innovation.

That's a mouthful. Here's what it really means:

3M allowed its people to make mistakes.

Employees are allowed to try new things. They are encouraged to break stuff and re-make it so it wouldn't break as easily. McKnight even demanded the company increase its mistakes by 10% the next year. Why? This is where innovation and creativity happens. It's a messy, sticky, and mistake-filled process going from idea to product development. Our dreams are no different. It's a long, bumpy, and circuitous path to success.

Clearly, one of the greatest traits of 3M's management culture is to delegate and allow people to make mistakes. The company thrives on unpredictability and failures – and those same failures led to path breaking innovations.

Goodwill

What's the first thing that comes into your mind when you think of Goodwill Industries? Most people think of the stores that sell donated goods at a very low price. When I was in college, this was where all the uber-cool, vampire-loving, retro-emo kids shopped.

As a part of my service to the local community, I will work with various non-profits in our local area. The two primary organizations I work with are Goodwill Industries and the Hunger Task Force. Both of these organizations share a building in Canton, Ohio. When residents are in need, they are able to request assistance from either organization for food and clothing.

Did you know that Goodwill Industries also provides job skills training and job placement services? Isn't that cool? Not only do they provide the clothes for jobs, they train and prepare adults to interview, and have employment agreements with local companies. The objective is to ensure that people are equipped with the basic math, reading, and computer skills to get a job. It's an incredible program and the dollars you spend and donate to Goodwill primarily go to support these types of services. But one of the first things they try to address is what people believe about themselves. You can dress right, say the right things, and even have the right skills, but you won't succeed if you don't have the right mindset.

The Power to Forgive Yourself

When there is a break in a relationship it is difficult to repair that connection without forgiveness. Even when both parties are justified in their views, and the truth is revealed, the only thing that melts the ice and allows full restoration is forgiveness.

This is true of your own life as well. Do you find it easier to forgive others, but not yourself? Do you hold on to past failures and regrets that keep you from moving forward?

Only you have the power to forgive yourself for past mistakes. Let them go. They belong to yesterday, not today.

Through Goodwill's job skills training and job placement services the number of people who are able to move on from receiving assistance to being able to support themselves is increasing. While those success stories are not the majority, they do happen.

There's a deeper story. The job market is challenging, the socio-economic surroundings are identical for all, and yet there are some people who are able to make it out. Almost everyone comes from a broken home and has fractured family relationships with little to no support structure. The problem also isn't a disparity in skill or intelligence. A significant number of these residents have at least graduated high school, so they went further than I did.

The primary culprit to their success is the belief that **they don't deserve it**. They've been beat down by life and don't expect to win. These are individuals defined by their past mistakes and feel it's inevitable to repeat their failures.

Is this you?

Believing in yourself is a process. It does not happen instantaneously. Remember, our minds are wired towards a negativity bias. Self-belief will look different for everyone. But it is critical in moving forward and progressing in your journey. If this is where you need to pause before you move on, then feel free to do that. Face it, given the limited knowledge and experiences you have, you will realize many more mistakes on your journey. At a certain point, you have to accept your past and that you've done everything in your power to amend what you can. You need to take those events as part of your story. This may be awkward and even painful, but this allows you to move on.

If you forgive yourself and learn from the past mistakes then you will have honored those experiences and it will be instructive going forward. Consider all the areas in which you've failed and now begin the process of learning from your blunders and creating a new path.

Get Rid of Those Jeans

I have a favorite pair of jeans. If I could, I would wear them all the time. But I can't. It's not appropriate to wear jeans everywhere unless you're Tim McGraw. Then I'd have to wear no shirt either, nobody needs that nonsense. A couple of years ago, I realized I had more than few of these 'favorites' still in my closet. Some were over 15 years old. There was no way I was going to fit into them.

But I hold on to them. Why? I think it's a combination of nostalgia, sentimentality, and a good ol' dose of pride. I looked good when I wore those jeans. I don't want to throw them out because what if I need to buy jeans again? If I simply lose a mere 40 lbs., I can easily slip back into those vice grips.

Just as important to stop kicking yourself over yesterday's failures, it's also essential to not rely on past successes.

Were you the best in your class? Perhaps your peak years were in high school? Mine weren't, *obviously*, but every school had their version of the Big Man on Campus. Were you an up-and-coming star in your department? Do you remember a time when you could do no wrong in your boss' eyes? Maybe you closed a great deal or invented a better way to do something but it's been several years since you've made any strides. You have to let those trophies go.

"But I like those trophies."

I get it. You did something great in the past. Huzzah. Holding onto past wins prevents you from taking chances in the future. If you were known as the one who could never fail, then you won't try new things. You'll be too afraid to make mistakes. You'll care too much about how people view you. Believe me, as one who thinks very highly of himself, even I have come to realize that people simply don't care that much. They're too busy worrying about their own lives to consider yours.

Like a pair of favorite jeans that don't fit anymore, it's time to let go of previous wins. Chuck them in yesterday's pile. They don't matter here today.

> **Past mistakes or previous wins do not impact today's success.**

Do you allow yourself this latitude?

Are you so worried about making a mistake that it freezes you from doing anything?

"I've missed more than 9000 shots in my career. I've lost almost 300 games. 26 times I've been trusted to take the game winning shot and missed. I've failed over and over and over again in my life. And that is why I succeed." – Michael Jordan

Who cares about your shooting percentage? Who cares you won 10 years ago?

We just want to know who wins the game today.

Keep shooting.

Chapter 2 Notes:

1. Morgan, L., G. Spreitzer, J. Dutton, R. Quinn, E. Heaphy, and B. Barker. (2005). How to Play to Your Strengths. Harvard Business Review, January 2005.
2. Morgan, L., G. Spreitzer, J. Dutton, R. Quinn, E. Heaphy, and B. Barker. (2005). How to Play to Your Strengths. Harvard Business Review, p.265.

"Do it, fix it, try it is our favorite axiom. Chaotic action is preferable to orderly inaction."

~ Tom Peters and Bob Waterman, *In Search of Excellence*

Chapter 3: Be a Fixer

Be Different

Everyone loves to complain. People complain about everything from their co-workers to the weather and traffic. When was the last time someone said, *"Boy, I'm sure glad it's taking us twice as long as I hoped to get to the beach."* No one in the history of man has said this. Admit it, we all complain.

Have you ever noticed how complaining impacts you?

It brings me down. Nothing lets the air out of the room like a groan and moan session. It never encourages me. When I complain or hear someone else complain, my immediate response is to join in. I want to be a part of the disgruntled crowd. In fact, I try to top someone else's complaint with an even better one of my own. It becomes a "wait until you hear this" type rivalry. Complaining begets more complaining.

Be different. Do something. Be a fixer.

Embrace Your Obstacles

Most people know Oprah Winfrey as one of the most iconic TV talk show hosts as well as one of the richest and most successful women in the world. She owns her own television network. Oprah faced a hard road to get to that position, however, enduring a tragically abusive childhood as well as numerous career setbacks including being fired from her job as a television reporter because she couldn't separate her emotions from her stories.

Not only did Oprah overcome her obstacles, she embraced them. She essentially created a new genre of daytime talk show hosting, where it became en vogue to be moved to tears while interviewing your guests. Oprah could have easily stayed within the status quo, she had endured more than most, but she was not content with being average or just getting by. She was resolved to be a success.

There are two choices in life when it comes to obstacles, you can give up or you can figure out a way around them.

What's Your Problem?

Being a fixer requires having a radical perspective.

According to Dictionary.com, the definition of **radical** literally means, "going to the root or origin; fundamental."

The objective is to identify the root issue of a problem, not just the symptoms.

When somebody complains that their problem is a lack of sales, what they're reporting is a symptom of a greater problem. If your sales aren't what you anticipated then simply lower the price. Problem solved. Here's my invoice.

Does this really solve the issue? Maybe, but more than likely there's a deeper complication that we are not addressing.

Poor sales numbers might reflect an over-priced product or could be the result of an ill-conceived marketing strategy. Do you even *have* a marketing strategy? Did you actually implement it? Could the problem be attributed to a lack of brand awareness? Does the product or service you're selling have tangible value to the consumer? Maybe your products are limited to region or season. Are the sales people properly incentivized to move your products or services?

Ask yourself this question: "If I gave my product or service away for free would customers be knocking down my door to get it?"

If you said no, then you may have to start at the beginning to make sure you have a product or service that meets customer demand.

Assess Before You Address

Stephen Covey, in his best-selling book, *The 7 Habits of Highly Effective People*, explains the pitfalls of trying to solve a problem before knowing the root cause. He calls it diagnosing the symptom before prescribing the medicine, or diagnose before you prescribe. Most people prescribe without diagnosis.

In the social media world, there are many opportunities to place our virtual feet in our mouths. Sites like Gawker and TMZ prove no one is exempt from being foolish on the Internet. There are studies that show people are less likely to be inhibited when using electronic media. This is further evidenced by the sheer volume of inappropriate texts, tweets, and Facebook posts every day.

You know what they say about making assumptions.

We have two little cherubs for children who never fight, argue, or misbehave. But on the rare occasion that our two boys decide to go at it, I've learned my lesson – don't intervene until first blood is drawn.

Actually no, I tend to get involved sooner than this because the yelling or crying reaches decibels where I am no longer able to maintain my sanity. But there have been too many times where I've stormed into a quarrel and sent one or both children to their rooms. I tend to lean my mercy towards whoever is crying harder.

I send the other one away. While this is easier and more expedient for me, I have not truly diagnosed the problem. I have not heard both sides. One child feels unheard and is less likely to trust and open up to me when I ask questions later on.

Too often I address the issue before I assess the situation. I jump to a solution without first diagnosing the problem. The result is a temporary reprieve but the problems return again because I have not addressed the root issue.

Real Cry vs. Fake Cry

Through my university, I was able to take my family to Italy for a month during the summer of 2013. It was glorious. On one of those picturesque moments where my wife and children were walking back to campus, the children were about 100 yards ahead of her off the beaten path. She could see they were jumping and screaming like they normally do. This is how our boys communicate, they jump and scream. Nothing out of the ordinary. But after a few seconds, she could see they were jumping higher and their screams became more frantic. Definitely a real cry.

She ran to see what the problem was. She saw huge, splotchy welts forming on their little legs. They had somehow walked into a patch of three feet high stinging nettles. If you haven't experienced this, it's like walking into a wasps' nest that's been sitting on the sun. Everywhere they turned there were more stinging nettles. The kids were hysterical; my wife was hysterical, it was a total mess. The stinging needles had now reached all the way up their little legs and they couldn't walk. She was alone so she had to carry each child individually the last half mile back to campus.

Thankfully they ended up being fine; after a few days the swelling went down. It was scary to think of having two young children in a foreign country with a horrible reaction to plant life you've never seen. It's even more frightening to think how quickly the squeals of delight went to desperate cries of pain. I would have never recognized it. They sound almost identical to me. Luckily my wife could tell the difference between a real cry and a fake one.

Don't assume you know what's going on because you've been in this situation before. I tell my students frequently, "Don't think you know the answer because you've heard the question a million times. There may be a twist to the question or the scenario."

Don't assume you know the solution because you've seen the problem before. Each problem is unique and deserves a fresh look.

Think like a Consultant

If you're familiar with the *Dilbert* comic strip, you know that consultants are often portrayed as overpriced charlatans. As a consultant, I'm here to tell you we're not overpriced.

In reality, the value of hiring an external consultant is the ability to leverage their knowledge, resources, and experience to help your company implement change or address a systemic problem. But what the consultant really brings to the table is an objective perspective and the ability to ask good questions. So why hire someone to do something you can do? Good question. Most try thinking like a consultant, but it's difficult to maintain objectivity when you're knee-deep in your problems.

Here's the key: Maintain an objective perspective and ask good questions.

In order to strategize and implement a solution, you need to first accurately assess the root cause.

Get to the Root Cause

Ask the 3 'W' questions:

1. **What** – What happened? Where did it happen? When did it happen? Get the facts. Ensure you get an objective account of the problem and the events that led to the problem. (Ex: One of your critical shipments is late from a key strategic vendor.)

2. **Who** – Who are the people involved? Often problems can arise because an employee was willingly or mistakenly not able to perform a task. (Ex: The receiving department employee entered the wrong shipping address.)

3. **Why** – Why did this happen? What process, policy, and practices are in place in order for people to do their jobs optimally? (Ex: The shipping code was not double-checked by a second employee to ensure the correct address.)

Refuse to give up until you find the root problem. Don't be fooled, if you don't find the root cause, you've simply treated the symptom, and the problem is likely to return. Don't mistake sticking a bandage for applying a true tourniquet. If the wound is deep, the bandage is only a temporary alternative.

Once you get to the root of the problem, you will have identified what the moving parts are, the various reasons of why this problem exists, and who the responsible parties are. You will now have a clearer idea of how to eliminate the problem and keep it from reoccurring.

If you believe something is a problem that needs to be solved, then it is. Obstacles, setbacks and failures are simply facts of life. The best thing you can do is to meet them with a problem solver mind-set.

Problem Finder

Are you finding the right problem?

Be careful not to rest on your laurels just because something works right now. Think of Polaroid, analog film, typewriters, VHS, and phonebooks – it was easy for these companies to continue working on their core competencies. In reality, were they really looking for a new problem? Or were they just simply solving problems they already knew the answers to? You may be relying on past successes to the detriment of your future dreams.

Have you ever heard of Burbn'?

Burbn' was a GPS-based location sharing mobile application developed by Kevin Systrom and Mike Krieger. Kevin and Mike launched Burbn' in 2010 with the help of some venture capitalists.

It never took off. The initial investment of $500K was going nowhere. People downloaded the app, but they weren't 'checking in' anywhere. But they noticed something as they looked at the analytics and how people were using Burbn'. The most used function of Burbn' was of people taking and sharing photos online. They solicited and actually listened to feedback from users, imagine that. They also paid close attention to the <u>actual numbers</u> of how their app was being used. They realized people loved posting and sharing their photos. They re-focused their efforts on building a better platform for posting and sharing pictures on the Internet.

Instagram was born 10 months later – they hit 1 million users in 3 months.

Kevin called that meeting with the development group his own 'pivot' moment. Instagram was acquired by Facebook in April 2012 for $1B. As of July 2014, there are now over 200 million active monthly users with over 20 billion photos shared.

They were asking the wrong question initially. *But they weren't afraid to dive deeper.*

"How can we create a great location-sharing app?" wasn't the right question for them.

After studying user feedback, seeing what people were using their products for, and scanning the existing competition (Hipstamatic and Facebook) they came up with a new question: **"How can we create a *simple* photo-sharing app?"**

Lessons learned from BURBN':

1. Sometimes you begin pursuing your solution without knowing what the real problem is.
2. Unless you start fixing stuff, you won't have a chance to take a deeper dive.
3. Don't be afraid to re-think your core competency.

Can We Simplify?

As managers and leaders, we can get enamored with the latest and greatest technology or management tool and risk matrices. We believe that being simple is just plain boring and unsophisticated. Of course these tools and resources have their place, but there is something powerful about seeking a more simple solution.

Steve Jobs' goal for Apple was to make his computers elegant and beautiful. How he did it was through simplicity. Jobs' objective was to distil the idea down to its essence. He felt that other companies tried to make things overly complex. He wanted simplification.

Notice how the iPhone, iPad, and iPod all have one centrally located home button. The iconic white ear buds became a symbol of cool technology that 'just works.' It just works the way it's supposed to work. Have you ever noticed how these devices have no instruction manuals or CD to install drivers? This is by design.

Other companies make the process overly complex. It makes the user feel stupid.

Apple's products are so simple they don't ever require instructions. This subconsciously forces the user to become their own tech support. You don't see instructions so the inherent message becomes, "It's so simple I can figure this out." This empowers the user.

How can you simplify?

Have one clear goal.

What is your one objective for your new product, service, or personal goal or dream?

Apple's is to design things so beautifully simple they just work. They don't make the customer think too hard. Amazon's goal is to be customer-obsessed. Google wants to organize the world's information.

Remove What Doesn't Fit

Have a laser-like focus on what your goal is. Eliminate all the peripheral things that get in the way of that target. Don't bog yourself down with additional features that are cool and 'add value'. This just muddies the water. Clear your mind and start cutting away the fat.

Strive for Consistency

If it's a sales incentive plan, have one plan that applies to all regardless of position or seniority. You want to reward based on performance now, not previous history. If we're talking technology, consider having one technology platform so that everyone has access to the same information. When communicating to your employees set a communication strategy and implement the plan consistently. This eliminates confusion, nepotism, and rumors.

> **"Success begets success."** ~ Unknown

The Virtuous Cycle

In economics, the virtuous cycle is a complex chain of events that reinforces itself through a feedback loop. Feedback loops reinforce the previous actions. The cycle of success begins with one area, but then quickly starts to impact another area of your life. This is the concept behind systems thinking as well. An organizational system or business process doesn't exist in a vacuum; neither do we as human beings. Our lives are a complex mesh of relationships, habits, and beliefs.

Dr. Nido Qubein, a world-renowned business leader, explains success as the ability to have intentional congruence. In other words how can you achieve the greatest return on your investment of time, money, and energy when your efforts are not connected in some way? Do things that you believe will have a positive impact on everything else.

Take, for example, when you are exercising, you begin to notice what you are eating. If I start my morning with a workout, I'm less likely to eat that extra cupcake. I also start drinking more water, which leads to more energy and less sitting. This then leads to weight loss, which motivates more morning workouts.

What's even more interesting?

I start to notice other areas of my life that will improve as well. I will write on a more consistent basis; I start finishing more of my projects. My mind is more in tune with my environment, and I am better able to engage my students and clients.

That is the power of the virtuous cycle. Improvement in one area starts to impact other areas and it starts the ball rolling.

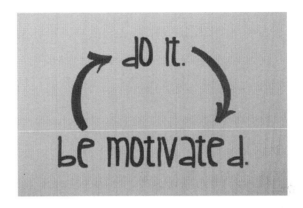

Jumpstart

Like a dead battery, we sometimes need a jumpstart to get going. We need to recharge the battery. It's not completely dead, it's just *mostly* dead.

What is one thing you can start doing today? What can you do to push that virtuous cycle to start? If you are at a complete standstill and have no motivation at all, these are some steps that will help.

Steps to a Jumpstart:

1. Start with something easy (ex: clean your office, desk, car, organize your desktop folders and files).
2. Start something that has a definite end date. Don't start your great American novel as your first thing to tackle. Ideally, this task should be finished within the same day you start. It's important to see the result the same day.
3. Tell somebody – even if you simply blog about it – it forces some level of accountability. Your action will be 'out there'

for someone else to see. Even if no one reads it, you are still on record as stating you will do it. Now do it.

Feedback Loop

In the software engineering environment, we need feedback loops built within our systems. For any software program to function, it needs data inputs which leads to data processing and then outputs, which serves as a feedback loop for additional inputs until the job is done.

All of the elements, inputs, processing, and outputs are necessary, but it doesn't make sense without feedback. The logic of the entire system is based on a feedback loop.

How gratifying is it when you do something positive and you get great feedback? Just like the chimpanzee that receives a preferred treat like grapes when it pulls on the blue lever as opposed to the bland cucumber when it pulls the red lever, the feedback loop reinforces a certain behavior. It motivates you to continue that action to repeat the reward. Positive feedback is necessary for positive action.

When you are starting your new goals, look for ways to get small and quick methods of positive feedback. You will need about four mistakes to get one success, so get busy trying things. When you increase the number of tries, you increase your number of successes.

Vicious Cycle

Unfortunately, the same is true of the Vicious Cycle. Remember the negativity bias? We are 4 times more likely to remember negative feedback than positive. So we need a ratio of 4:1 for positive feedback in our virtuous cycle.

When it comes to the Vicious Cycle, doing nothing is worse than doing something wrong.

Let me say it another way: doing something poorly is still better than no action at all.

At least when you do something badly, you have the benefit of learning from the mistake. You are still getting feedback, but now you can ask others for input on how to do things differently. If you do nothing, there is no learning. You just feel guilty, which leads to anxiety, panic, and more nothing. Stop doing nothing.

Finish Stuff

One way to break the vicious cycle is to finish things. When I think about all of the different things I need to do and take care of on my list it can get pretty overwhelming and discouraging.

If you're anything like me, you can even invent new ways to do other stuff, before do the things you really need to do. My kids are pros at this. They can make these incredibly elaborate ways to prepare the bins for cleaning up their toys. The bins, steps, couch, and lights have all been booby-trapped and ready for massive clean-up, but they still haven't cleaned up the toys. They missed the main thing.

The Main Thing

I like what Tim Ferris, author of *The 4-Hour Workweek*, has to say about this. He says to ask yourself this question everyday:

"If this is the only thing I accomplish today, will I be satisfied with my day?"

In other words, what's the main thing you need to get done today?

You know what it is. It's the thing that's been nagging and gnawing at the back of your mind as you're trying to finish other 'important' things.

And if it's a choice between two or more legitimately important tasks, go back to Ferris' question, "If this is the only thing I accomplish today, will I be satisfied with my day?"

Tim goes on to explain, "If you haven't already accomplished at least one important task in the day, don't spend the last business hour returning a DVD to avoid a $5 late charge. Get the important task done and pay the $5 fine."[1]

You'll feel much more satisfied after you complete the main thing.

Time to celebrate, but only **after** you've finished. Have a latte. On me. Actually on Tim's dime, he can afford it.

> **"Many of life's failures are people who did not realize how close they were to success when they gave up."**
>
> **~ Thomas Edison**

Don't Give Up!

Have you ever felt like giving up?

I definitely have. Most mornings one of the first things I think is, *Boy do I love sleep. I can't wait to get back into that bed.* Almost every day, the first urge I have is to give up. The diet, the writing, the business, all of the work I still have yet to do. It would be so much easier just to check out and watch hours of YouTube. Don't do it. Don't give in to that way of thinking. Here are some ways that help remind me not to give up.

> **It's not that I'm so smart; it's just that I stay with problems longer.**
> ~ Albert Einstein

Kill Your Lazy

If you are not actively pursuing your goals, it is very easy to stay put. Like your TV couch, this a comfortable place to be. You know where everything is. You're not moving. The truth is, however, that you're actually drifting away. All that time not pursuing your goals is actually taking you further away from your dreams. Don't think of it like you're on the ground floor, waiting to go up. Think of it more like the ocean. Have you tried to stand in one spot in the ocean? You think you haven't moved, but the current has taken you further away from your original standing point. The sand beneath you is moving. It doesn't seem like you've moved because you haven't done anything. But when you try to find your beach chair and the rest of your family, you're already in Mexico.

Stop drifting.

Most people, when stressed, anxious, or overwhelmed by unfinished projects, tend to default to a state of inaction.

This is not unusual. It's called laziness. Harsh reality, but in order to achieve your dreams, you need to actively kill your laziness. Don't fall for the lie that doing nothing keeps you at the same place. It's okay to take a breather every now and again. Everyone does. But after that break, it's time to get back on the steps and start climbing.

It's not where you stop that determines your destination. It's where you quit.

> **"Losers quit when they're tired. Winners quit when they've won." ~ Unknown**

Make it Visual

Another technique that moves you to action is to make things visual. What is it that you need to do that you're not doing? Can you visualize it? Many professional athletes often credit their success on the field to their ability to envision their success off of it. Seeing your progress is a great way to jumpstart your virtuous cycle.

Are you competitive? Can you track your progress on a chart and hang it up on your wall? You can codify it in such a way that only you understand. Having a visual representation of what you're going to pursue is a fun and tangible way to see your progress and spur you on to keep going.

A creative exercise that I'm doing now for this book is writing out my main ideas onto index cards and then laying those cards out on my table to see what themes pop out. Not all the cards will make it, but I can save some of that material for my blog or for the next book.

I stole this idea from Austin Kleon's book *Steal Like An Artist.*

It didn't require a lot of heavy lifting. It's a physical representation of what's going on in my mind. I can track it as often as I want. I can move things around. It's like trying to fit pieces into a puzzle. I just took another step in the right direction.

What small steps can you visualize towards achieving your goal?

What can you do to make it fun so you stick with it longer?

Have you heard of vision boards? It's like Pinterest, but in real life.

Make your own vision board. It's fabulous. Make your board clearly visible so you are able to see your goals, action steps, and small wins every day. When it comes to success habits, seeing is believing.

Chapter 3 Notes:

1. Ferris, T. (2007). *The 4-Hour Workweek*, p.83.

> "Many ideas grow better when transplanted into another mind than the one where they sprang up."
>
> ~ Oliver Wendell Holmes

Chapter 4: Be a Serial Collaborator

We get more done when we work with other people. Nothing gets me more energized or enthusiastic about pursuing goals and dreams than meeting someone else who is like-minded or is pursuing their own dreams. The more I am able to involve other people in my dreams, visions, and goals, the more I come to realize them. Conversely, nothing gets me down and ruins my mojo as much as an *Eeyore*. Every group has one. An Eeyore is an individual who does nothing but complain, lacks vision, and can only focus on how hard things are. Avoid Eeyores at all costs.

Who's On Your Team?

A couple of years ago, I had a meeting with an 'entrepreneurial coach' and it was complete let down. I was so excited to meet this person. This coach was notoriously hard to schedule. This meeting took months to plan, so I was extremely excited for the opportunity to meet him.

I had some great ideas for a board game, and napkin drawings for inventing a household product. I was hoping this initial coaching session would lead to new opportunities. I had visions of meeting with venture capitalists or manufacturers to prototype my products. At the very least I hoped to expand my network to include other like-minded entrepreneurs or inventors. The meeting did not go the way I wanted. Not even close.

Even if nothing came out of the meeting, I was at least expecting to get a conversation filled with great ideas, thoughts, and critiques. I wasn't looking for a pat on the back; I really wanted to get some actionable feedback that I would be able to implement. I wanted a mentor or coach who would inspire to me further action.

What I got was a total let down. This 'coach' berated me for wasting his precious time. He demanded to know who I was and how I even secured this meeting. He didn't even look at my drawings or ideas. Here was the sum of our twenty minute discussion. He charged me with a few questions that sounded more like accusations:

"Do you realize how busy I am? I don't have time for this."

"Do actually you know how hard it is to produce a product?"

"I've seen plenty of people in your situation with 'good' ideas and they are all now broke."

Man, talk about a downer.

Don't get me wrong, I think it's important to have people ask you good and hard questions. The best take away for me was I really did need to go back to the drawing board for some of my ideas. I also needed to make sure I did a more extensive market analysis before pursuing other manufacturing or prototyping services.

It ended there. I was completely deflated. I didn't walk away with any solid action steps or leads for further contacts. Including my commute, there were two hours I could have spent doing something more productive.

Don't misinterpret this that I only want to surround myself with 'yes' people and need my ego stroked. I think there is a difference between offering constructive, critical, and thought-provoking questions versus spewing forth discouraging, disparaging, and how-can-you-be-so-stupid type questions. I was a nobody to this person, and he treated me accordingly.

I thought, "Hey, I'm the one who set this meeting up, took time out of my day, drove over to meet with you and now I'm getting berated. Where did I go wrong?"

This can happen from time to time. It challenged me to re-think what I wanted to do. It made me re-focus on what my goals and objectives were.

That's the advantage of meeting with other people who have a different perspective than you. Even if it isn't a good experience, you can still learn from it. It also taught me the importance of paying everyone the same level of respect regardless of their background, experience, or position in life.

Mastermind Group

The concept of the 'mastermind alliance' was formally introduced by Napoleon Hill in his best-selling book, *Think and Grow Rich.* Hill wrote about the Mastermind group principle as the joining of two or more people who work together with a common purpose. He says that:

"No two minds ever come together without thereby creating a third, invisible intangible force, which may be likened to a third [mastermind]."[1]

I couldn't find one locally, so I started my own Mastermind Group at work this past year. I wanted entrepreneurial colleagues to come in and have the freedom to share their ideas, thoughts, and goals in a safe and encouraging environment, without the fear of harsh judgments and criticisms. I think there is a time and a place to look at things critically, but the beginning stages of dream seeking and goal setting is not a place to stifle your visions. I reached out to four other colleagues and we started this past year.

I wanted this group to be a place where people could come openly with grand ideas, dreams, and goals. Even though we come from different disciplines and expertise, we are all college professors with the common purpose of improving our lives and pursuing our aspirations. While we are primarily focusing on our own personal goals, this Mastermind Group is also where relationships and trust are built and our personal networks can cross-pollinate and grow exponentially.

Great ideas are shaped and sharpened within the framework of relationships built on trust. You have to be able to trust your team.

Who do you have on your team?

The Wisdom of the Crowd

James Suroweicki wrote a book entitled *The Wisdom of the Crowd*. Here's the scene: imagine you're at the annual county fair in the early 1900s. There is an incredibly popular contest: guess the weight of a cow and you get to take it home! It only costs a few pennies to enter so you, along with over 750 people, take a look at the cow, guess a number, and put your wager in. The county fair is a pretty big deal, so it's going to draw in people from all walks of life from farmers and butchers, to doctors and lawyers, and everyone else you can think of. Given the multitude of differing opinions, expertise, and backgrounds you figure you have as good of a shot as anybody.

After the winners are announced, you realize you didn't win – but you're curious as to what the actual weight was. The cow's weight was 1,197 lbs. Not even close to your guess of 500 lbs.

If you were to average all 787 entries, the mean weight guess was 1,198 lbs. That is one pound off from the cow's actual weight!

Even more interesting, there were a few cow experts within the group and they couldn't guess the correct weight even within 100 lbs. But the collective intelligence of the group narrowed it down to a one pound difference.

Have you tried to figure out the problem in isolation? It's hard. You only get one viewpoint. Your likelihood of solving the problem relies solely on your individual expertise, energy, and persistence.

The benefit of having multiple perspectives trumps the ability of a select few 'experts' who think they know the answer.

This is the power of a large and diverse crowd.

Crowdsourcing

Crowdsourcing provides a way for individuals and organizations to access the wisdom, talent, and resources of the 'crowd', or online population.

Consider the following sites that allow you to access other people's talent like never before:

1. **Bandcamp** (connects the consumer and the artist without the middle man)
2. **Kickstarter/Indiegogo/GoFundMe/RocketHub** (crowd funding site that allows entrepreneurs, artists, musicians, non-profits to pitch an idea to the crowd for funding opportunities)

3. **Quirky** (crowd-inventing that allows your invention idea come to actual production stage and retail if it's popular enough and has enough 'pre-sales' from the crowd)
4. **Spiceworks** (IT and Management people coming together to access the collective intelligence of IT workers everywhere)
5. **E-Lance** (propose a freelance job and select from the best across the world)
6. **Fiverr** (propose small jobs like designing an e-book cover or setting up a landing page, for as low as $5 per gig)
   a. Note most of the cooler projects on fiverr.com cost a little more than $5. The cover and spine design for this book was only $15. I think this was a much better use of my money than spending a few weeks trying to design my own cover.

Synergy

Synergy has been abused as a management buzzword, but the actual definition comes from the Greek word *Synergos* which means 'working together.' Synergy happens when the sum of the whole system is greater than the sum of its individual parts.

For example, if you are a consultant bringing in $1 million of revenue and you decide to collaborate with an equal consulting partner that also brings in $1 million, the resulting merger should be significantly greater than $2M total. Or else this isn't synergy.

Synergy is capitalizing on areas of strength and limiting weakness in order to increase the revenue for both of you. In this instance 1 + 1 should equal 3 or else it's not worth it.

Diversity Trumps Ability

In 1962 a pretty good drummer by the name of Ringo replaced incumbent drummer Pete Best, and joined three other relatively unknown amateur musicians from Liverpool, England. They played hours upon hours in Hamburg, Germany, honing their set, sound, look, and stage presence and eventually the Beatles became the most accomplished rock-n-roll band in history selling over 250 million records.

By all accounts, the four 4 musicians individually were talented, but when they came together (yes, pun intended) synergy magic happened. Synergy only occurs when the collective and diverse talents of the team trump their individual abilities.

Most successful people do not simply pursue individual accomplishments. Rather, they cultivate and leverage the diversity and strength of their team to get more done than they ever could alone.

The collective intelligence of the group has an advantage over the single problem solver because many different perspectives lead to more potential solutions. A diverse group of reasonably capable problem solvers can often outperform a group composed entirely of experts.

There is a synergistic effect when we collaborate with others. We not only get more done, it's a lot more fun, challenging, creative, and we come up with a better end product. Who are you working with these days?

Communities of Practice

Are you a part of a community of practice? A community of practice provides a safe and nurturing environment in which people can pursue learning, development, and growth within their areas of expertise of industry.

At my university we have Faculty Learning Communities (FLCs) that do this very thing. We meet once or twice a month and we discuss what works and what doesn't work in the classroom. While I am in the School of Business, we may get faculty members from Nursing, Biology, English, and Education. The diversity of the FLC provides valuable content and insights we couldn't have if it were just business faculty.

How often do you actively pursue networking opportunities outside of your department, office, or building? When learning opportunities are offered, such as conferences, seminars, lunch and learns, and Chamber of Commerce events, are you actively engaged?

It is important to participate in a community of practice if you want to grow.

Saddle Up, Partner

Who are you collaborating with to achieve more success? Here's an idea, partner with the nearest local university as a creative hub. What more diverse group of people could there be in a small, focused area?

At our small university in Northeast Ohio, we have over 120 full-time faculty, over 300 adjunct faculty, and a fairly diverse student population of over 2,500 including graduate and international students.

Speaking of students, consider hiring students as paid or unpaid interns for your business. They are eager for knowledge and experience and you may get some really great perspectives you haven't previously considered.

Even small college towns have experienced strong economic growth through a partnership with their local universities. Pittsburgh, Pennsylvania, has transitioned itself from an industrial (steel/coal-based) economy to a knowledge-based economy (technology, world-class universities, and health care) through partnerships with the University of Pittsburgh, Robert Morris University, Carnegie Mellon University, and a handful of other schools that have contributed to the knowledge base there.

Train Them Up

How many young people do you employ, mentor, or train? There is a strong correlation between active employee training and development and retention of talent. This is especially true of younger associates. Provide training and cross-training for them. You will reap many additional benefits. Younger and less-seasoned workers are more prone to ask questions and more willing to take risks. Now is the time for them to do this while they are learning their new skills and their responsibility load is lighter.

Creative clusters tend to congregate towards other creative clusters. This is also true of younger people. They tend to congregate together. So if you want to attract good and young talent, you will have to retain your good and young talent.

Be sure to let them work on complex and meaningful problems. People need to work on problems that are challenging and have some meaning of significance. Even more than money or external motivators, employees want to know their work means something. They want to know and feel they are actually contributing value as opposed to doing menial work simply for a paycheck.

The old way of managing and working with teams was to emphasize conformity and adherence to a code. You pay your dues, do your time, and follow the company line and only then will you be rewarded after 30 years of loyalty and servitude.

The new information and knowledge economy favors individuality and different ways of thinking of the same old problems. Today's knowledge workers seek personal enrichment goals, the acceptance of differences, and the desire for diverse and rich multi-cultural experiences and people.

It's important to recognize and celebrate different skills and backgrounds when conducting team projects and creating new work groups.

Mash-ups

A mash-up is combining one key element from one source with another element from another source. Chefs, artists, and musicians do this all the time. Have you ever tried apples with cheese, pretzels with anything sweet, or peanut butter and bacon? Actually anything with bacon. My favorite mashup is bacon with bacon. Have you listened to the Jay-Z and Toto mash-up of 'Africa?' Not normally a fan of Jay-Z, but this is pretty cool. Vanilla Ice's uber-hit song 'Ice Ice Baby' was a re-mix of 'Under Pressure' by Queen.

Business Mash-ups

Even combining seemingly unrelated things can lead to incredible results.

Have you ever had to use a multi-list to look for real estate? Combining Google maps and real estate data on housing prices led to Zillow. Combining the social network aspect of Facebook with professional businesses and job seekers led to the incredibly popular LinkedIn professional network site. Combining cloud computing and file storage led to Dropbox.

Challenge Your Assumptions

Scientists in Korea are using the AIDs virus to kill cancer cells in the lungs. The modified virus halted the progression of lung cancer without damaging the healthy cells.

Timothy Brown, AKA 'The Berlin Patient,' was diagnosed with HIV in 1995 and then Leukemia 10 years later. As he underwent a bone marrow transplant for his leukemia, Dr. Gero Huetter, a German hematologist, was able to conduct the transplant using donated bone marrow that had a 'CCR5 delta 32' gene mutation that was resistant to HIV.

This innovative procedure not only caused the patient to be cancer-free but also HIV-free for five years. They have effectively concluded that the cure of HIV infection has been achieved for this patient. Several years later two men in Baltimore also underwent the innovative treatment and were cured of their HIV as well.

Combining the two unrelated treatments has caused a ground-breaking cure for a previously incurable disease.

Did you know this is how the term vaccination was created?

The first vaccination was developed by Edward Jenner in 1796. Jenner had noticed that those who suffered from cowpox (mild illness) were immune to the much more deadly smallpox (killed thousands). So by injecting children with cowpox, he eliminated the smallpox disease. In fact, the term vaccination comes from the Latin term 'vaccinia' meaning cow.

3M and Google

Former 3M CEO, William McKnight learned a crucial lesson about letting his engineers follow their instincts. He soon transformed this lesson into a policy known as the 15% rule. "Encourage experimental doodling," he told his managers. "If you put fences around people, you get sheep. Give people the room they need."

Still in place today, the 15% rule lets 3M engineers spend up to 15% of their work time pursuing whatever project they like.

Google's Pareto Principle

Google's culture was heavily influenced by McKnight's management philosophy. You've probably heard of the Pareto Principle where 80% of your sales come from the top 20% of your customers. Most call this the 80/20 rule. Google's variation of the Pareto Principle encourages its Google engineers to spend 20% of their time working on their own creative ideas. This allows the engineers to work outside of their departments and collaborate with other areas one out of every five days. Google's 80/20 rule has led to over 50% of its most recent products including some of its most popular services such as Gmail, Google Maps, and AdSense.

Both 3M and Google not only allow collaboration to happen, they require it. They require their engineers to work with people from outside their departments, like marketing and sales, or pairing people from collections to help out with customer service training.

Collaboration forces you to consider a problem from another person's perspective. When someone doesn't know your particular discipline, they will ask you some interesting questions that you probably had not considered.

Unexpected or unusual questions require you to think before you speak. This forces you to go back to the basics. It gets you to truly consider what you know and what you don't know. Don't worry, this is a good thing. If you have a strong team, these are the problems you want to tackle.

Collaboration also makes you reflect how your actions might impact others. You are not only responsible for your own achievements; you are now hitched to another person's success. Team success is easier to achieve, more fun, and the results are almost always going to be better.

It's also important to encourage people to take their own initiative.

The McKnight Principle states:

"Management that is destructively critical when mistakes are made kills initiative. And it's essential that we have many people with initiative if we are to continue to grow."

Great collaboration is about flat structures where people do what they love doing, are independent and do not hesitate in making mistakes. Initiative only comes with independence – and the McKnight Principle testifies to this profound truth.

As managers, the lesson here is to never be over-critical about mistakes your team makes – it just pushes your people away from taking initiatives. All you have then is a bunch of 'do-as-directed' people who fear taking initiatives. It's no fun managing such a team, and no fun working for such a manager.

One Simple Idea

Stephen Key, the inventor of Lazer Tag, and the Teddy Ruxpin doll, has some excellent tips to creative collaboration, especially in the area of retail and commercialization of products. His specialty is coming up with new products or solutions.

His main argument is that you should focus on simple ways to fix things. This is often what resonates most with consumers. What is one simple idea you can implement today that can help you solve a problem, create a new product or service, or get more customers?

He essentially asks three questions:

1. Can I mix and match? (ex: Mickey Mouse shaped ice tray)
2. What If? (ex: What if I could tie my shoe with just one hand?)
3. How can I solve this problem? (ex: How can I prevent bacon neck on my undershirts?)

Sustainable Success

In improvisational acting there is a common tool called the "No Buts, Yes And" rule. You work with an improv partner and everything they say is permissible. You cannot say No or But; you have to say Yes and And. This forces you to weave your partner's story into your own narrative.

You take turns moving the story forward and it continues until you can't go anymore or the story concludes. What is fascinating is how unique and interesting the stories become when you have two participants that are open to each other's suggestions.

Be open to working with people who are different to you.

You might be surprised and learn something. Everyone contributes and everyone wins. This is sustainable success.

Chapter 4 Notes:

1.   Hill, Napoleon. (1937). *Think and Grow Rich.*

"The time to act is now."

~ Unknown

Chapter 5: Doing Is the New Thinking

Start Now

No great thing has been ever been achieved without taking that first step. The momentum of the start is so important for beginning stages. There has to be not just a strong desire, *but a burning desire.* A desire that burns so bright that even the 5AM alarm, the crying kids, or hundreds of other obstacles around you can't snuff it out.

What do you have a burning desire for?

Is it time to start a new chapter in your life? Do you want to pursue a new business or career opportunity? Perhaps it's something that you've never thought possible before. This is a good place to start. Think big.

Best-selling author, Brian Tracy asks, "What would you dream if you never thought you could fail?" I love this question. What is it that you so desperately/secretly want to do and accomplish in this life but are too scared of failing? That's your dream. It starts with a burning desire. Burning desire leads to action. But it only happens if you start.

So what's holding you back?

Wasting Time Wastes Time

Take a moment and think about your day. Recall all of the tasks and things you were able to accomplish.

Consider these statements:

"I really used my time well today."

"I got everything done that I needed to and I was able to prepare for tomorrow's tasks."

Is this you?

If you're being honest, this is probably not the case most of the time.

Now think about your week. If you think your *day* was wasted, consider all of the time you weren't productive during the *entire week*.

We are on information overload. Everything from smartphone apps, emails and Facebook, to office gossip and small talk can lead to a time drain, even if it's only for a few minutes. Let's go back to Monday. You have every intention to finally finish that report that your boss needs for the quarterly board meeting.

You have your mind set on being done today by noon.

The second you login you see you have 50 new email messages. Well you better check them because they could be important, right? You browse through and you find a few easy ones you can delete, but you've been waiting to hear back from this certain friend on the status of the problem you talked about two weeks ago. You have to just read through these emails and then you'll start that report.

A colleague comes in asking you if you have any information on the Smith file. You pride yourself in being a team player, so of course you review your documents to make sure you have it. You want to provide a photocopy of the files, and since it will only take a few minutes, you figure *I'll just do this myself. I don't want to bother the admin staff.* Your copy just jammed the machine. You need to call the helpdesk because this is your problem now.

You finally get it fixed, files copied, crisis averted.

Someone liked one of your posts on Facebook. Good, people are recognizing your genius. But an acquaintance of another 'friend' leaves a snarky comment that contradicts your status. This just got real.

You're smarter than this, so you're not going to respond right away. That's bush league. But in the meantime, you've totally lost track of what the objective was for your Monday morning board meeting.

Wasting Time Kills Momentum

You may have the best of intentions to get that report, project, or assignment done today, but if you keep getting distracted *you have to start from scratch every time you go back to the task.* Our brains can't handle the constant interruptions.

The brain has to re-align itself to the task.

Like a sprinter who takes a water break at every turn, you don't have the benefit of riding the wave of momentum when you stop. You have to expend a lot of energy just to re-start! Don't stop at every turn. Take a break when you need it, but too many time wasting distractions kills momentum.

It's Your Time

Take ownership of your time. Much like you would with your money or your possessions. Everyone gets the same 168 hours in a week, make sure you allocate those precious hours to something productive and dream building. Time draining activities not only take up time, they also kill any momentum you've built up to finish your goal.

Here's a simple exercise for you to try this week: Finish something important to you before you take a break or move on to another project. It could be anything, but it must have a significant meaning for your goals.

Why We Procrastinate

Have you ever thought of why we procrastinate?

This is such an interesting aspect of human behavior to me. We all do it. We all know we do it and recognize its detrimental effects on our lives and productivity, and yet we still engage.

"In psychology, procrastination refers to the act of replacing high-priority actions with tasks of lower priority, or doing something from which one derives enjoyment, and thus putting off important tasks to a later time"[1]

Another study classifies procrastination as having one or three of these characteristics:

1. Counterproductive
2. Needless
3. Delaying

Those are some great descriptions for a few of your co-workers, aren't they? Admit it, right now you have someone in mind that fits that description to a tee. Stop. Let's turn the mirror back to you.

This may not be a pleasant exercise, but honestly ask yourself, *Is what I'm doing right now in any way going to be counterproductive, needless, or delay me from my goal?*

Distraction is a beguiling mistress. There are times when you go from meeting to meeting, respond to multiple emails, grab a quick bite before you realize you haven't done anything that you get paid to do.

Then when you do have some downtime you feel entitled to spend the next 3 to 300 minutes surfing online, Facebooking, Pinning, and playing whatever version of Angry Birds they have today.

Ask Yourself 2 Questions:

#1. What is it that I need to be doing right now to get closer to my goal/objective?

THEN...

#2. Is what I'm doing right now taking me closer to that goal or task?

If you answered NO to question #2, you need to re-consider what you're doing.

Do the Most Important Thing First

This is often a technique I employ if I am behind or just simply not having any success getting things done.

It's not something I always do, but I think it should be a tool in your 'get stuff done' toolbox.

Of all the things you need to do/get done/accomplish/whatever, rank them from most important to least.

Leave the fluffy stuff for later, to do only after you've tackled the big stuff. There's going to be a temptation to knock out one easy thing off your list so you can at least say you got something done. If you are a natural procrastinator, don't do it.

If time management is your weakness, then this is a good technique for you.

Feel the pressure of having no check marks on your list <u>until</u> you get the most important thing done.

Here was my list for this weekend:

1. Finish course development for my online MBA class.
2. Grade student papers (20 students x 15 pp = 300 pp).
3. Schedule Assignments/due dates/project deadlines for the rest of the semester and re-organize the course calendar.
4. Draft letter to send to speakers/experts to participate in the Entrepreneurship Fair.
5. Get ice cream.

Guess which one I did first?

If you know me, you'd say #5, but I didn't. I immediately started on #1 – finish writing my curriculum for my MBA course. And I kept going until I was done. There were moments when I thought, *I'm just going to start going down the list,* but I stopped myself from deviating from the plan. And then I moved #5 all the way up to #2.

Do the most important thing first. And you know what happened? I started enjoying the process. I realized this wasn't a huge insurmountable mission. I started to see some tiny gains and recognized it was possible because I was breaking it down to one module at a time. Remember the power of small wins. It was painful, but each module I completed, I was able to do the next one just a little quicker. I had momentum and I was reducing the learning curve each time I completed a task.

Doing Is the New Thinking

I noticed my confidence rising as I went on. As I was doing the work, I was more aware of what I was completing. It's almost like having an out of body experience. When you are working on completing a task, and your mind, body, and consciousness are all congruently aligned to complete the task, you become better at it.

And then you start to think of ways to improve what you're doing. You're doing and thinking at the same time. It generates an environment of productivity and creativity to complete the task. I also felt the exhilaration of accomplishing something important. *But you can only think and do while you're in the midst of doing.*

It's important to do work that matters. And usually the work that matters is not so quick and easy to finish. As you're trudging through the muck to get done, be sure to look for ways to make the process even better or easier the next time.

It's important to start now. Do the one thing you've been putting off all week.

Keep working at it, even if it's just for a little bit. Get that boulder moving in the right direction.

> **"Do it. Then you will be motivated to do it."**
>
> **~ Zig Ziglar**

What Do You Want to Do?

This is a great question that I've asked many people in their journey to help them 'find' themselves.

Do you have a great idea to start or improve your business? Are you on the cusp of a new mobile app development startup?

How long have you been sitting on the sidelines waiting for your turn to get in the game? Don't fall into the myth of 'perfect time'; the time to act is now. Whether you are a young entrepreneur or a seasoned veteran, stop over-thinking and start doing.

As a college professor, I have the opportunity to advise many students who are both in and outside of my classes. I love career advising time. The opportunities are boundless and the dreams are big. I want to cultivate that in my students.

Dream big, or else why else are you here? You can get an education anywhere, but you're here now. So what would you love to start doing?

Jon Acuff, in his book *Start*, asks another question.

Not only what would I love to start doing, but what can I NOT STOP doing now?

That is, what in your life experiences points you to a place where you are most naturally you? What lights up your life? What work, music, hobbies, books, movies, extracurricular activities, and people light up your imagination and creativity? What do you find yourself doing naturally and losing all sense of time when you do it?

I have a few friends who love gaming. I mean LOVE gaming. When they are playing their games, they lose all sense of time and reality. They even skip meals. Why would anyone skip food? I've never done this. I eat the meals these guys miss.

Now does that mean you should run and find a career in videogames? Not necessarily. But perhaps it means you have a natural knack of computing systems, or application programming, or mobile app development. Or maybe you really should pursue your call to be a full-time gamer.

What it really means is that, while we're looking for our true passion to start doing something, we should take a moment and observe what we already do.

So what is it that you cannot stop doing?

What would you do if you had to do it for free?

This might be the key to finding what you were made for.

I love speaking and teaching. I love laughing, socializing, and learning from other people.

It's probably a prerequisite of all college professors and professional speakers, but I really do love speaking and teaching. In every life circumstance in some measure I am either speaking or teaching to an audience. While it doesn't happen every time, I usually try to incorporate some level of humor or levity in my speaking. I believe it's the one of the best ways that people will remember what you're sharing.

As a consultant I use my past experience and knowledge to help companies manage their organizational environment or implement new changes. Every client I have is another opportunity to learn while doing. I ask lots of questions. Even when I understand the scenario, I will still ask questions to make sure I didn't miss anything, but also because I tend to glean from someone else's perspective whom I haven't heard from before. Believe it or not, when you ask the same exact question to the CEO and one of the line supervisors of the same company, you can get vastly different answers.

What are some of the areas in your life that attract you?

Based on your natural interests and inclinations, can any of those interests, hobbies, or skills relate to a new dream or goal?

Take some time this week and give this some deeper thought and consideration.

Chapter 5 Notes:

1. Procrastination. (2014). In Wikipedia. Retrieved on August 2, 2014 from http://en.wikipedia.org/wiki/Procrastination.

> "Success is achieved by developing our strengths, not by eliminating our weaknesses."

> ~ Marilyn vos Savant

Chapter 6: Focus on Your Strengths

In order to achieve optimal performance, you need to focus on your strengths. Too many people spend too much money, time, and effort trying to fix things that are "broken." Here's the secret – you aren't broken. You are exactly who you were meant to be. Your talents, interests, and abilities as well as your flaws, incapacities, and oddities are all uniquely yours. Are there areas of improvement? Sure, but you can't fundamentally change who you are. This is akin to changing your DNA. It's impossible. You can actively do things to change your physical appearance: lose or gain weight, change hair color, get teeth and vision corrections, but none of those outside modifications change your core DNA.

Don't try to become a different you. Focus on becoming a better you.

Don't Overcome a Weakness

Concentrating on areas of weakness is actually an unrewarding time drain. Why focus on trying to change something that is not naturally your strength? When you constantly try to work on your mistakes and fix your failures, it actually leads to more failure. Here's why: It takes longer to learn a new skill than it does to hone an existing one. Besides being a time-waster, it takes you away from creatively expounding upon your current capabilities. Your lack of immediate results will sap your enthusiasm.

Hack-A-Shaq

Remember former NBA All-Pro Center Shaquille O'Neal? He splashed onto the scene with the Orlando Magic and quickly became a superstar for the league. He was so much bigger and stronger than everyone else he just muscled his way to the hoop for an easy bucket.

His weakness? He was a notoriously bad free throw shooter. He knew it. The opponents knew it. His mother knew it. Shaq missed so many free throws (over 5,300 – only the second player in NBA history to reach this mark[1]) that other teams started implementing a defensive strategy called "Hack-A-Shaq." Opposing teams would rather give up a foul and force O'Neal to the charity stripe than give him an opportunity to score. He made a little over half (52%) of his free throws. The average free throw shooting percentage for all 30 teams is 75.7%. This means Shaq would have to make a 50% improvement over his current weakness just to be average.

Now imagine if Shaq spent all of his time practicing his free throws? Would the return on the investment of time be worth the return on performance on the court?

Hall of Fame Lakers coach Phil Jackson didn't think so. Jackson explained that Shaq would never be an 80-90% free throw shooter. So why bother trying to spend a majority of his time fixing a weakness that will never become a strength?

In 2001, Jackson asked O'Neal to focus on areas of strength: lifting weights and getting stronger, better footwork and defensive positioning, and improving his incredible low-post offense. In his

21 seasons in the NBA, his highest free throw shooting percentage was during that 2002 season, where he shot over 62%. Almost 10% higher than his career average. Shaq also won his third straight NBA Championship and Finals MVP Award that year equaling Michael Jordan as the only player to win three consecutive NBA Finals MVP Awards.

None of the areas of strength that Shaq worked on involved shooting more free throws. Coach Jackson knew at best he would be below average when it comes to making free throw shots. Yet he had plenty of other areas to work on that made him exceptional. When you work and focus on your strengths – even your weaknesses can improve as an ancillary benefit.

Stock Control

In the manufacturing world, there is a term called Stock Control. It's when a business establishes a baseline level of inventory to determine an accurate record of how much product it currently has. This allows management to strategically plan and ensure there are enough products to meet consumer demand.

This is an important step in focusing on your strengths. It's time to take an inventory of your skill set. What are you good at? What attracts you? What do you inherently enjoy doing?

When you focus on your strengths, you are able to do work that is more enjoyable. You are working from a position of peak capacity.

Fully Engaged

Can you remember a time in your life when you were fully engaged with an activity? Remember when you lost all sense of time and got lost in your work? This is what happens when you are focusing on your strengths. You see things more clearly. Your senses are sharper. You are more engaged with your work.

You are more creative and your senses come alive.

Isn't this the kind of work that you want to be doing?

People around you start to notice and they want to work with you. You begin to create better relationships as you collaborate.

What's Missing?

Sometimes it's hard to think of areas where you're great. Many people have a hard time assessing their strengths. If you had strict parents or a challenging childhood, this is probably true for you.

If someone were to ask you to think of three areas you need to improve, you could probably rattle off a list of ten. But think of areas of competence, and self-doubt rears its ugly head. It's almost like we need to be given permission to think positively about ourselves.

It's been said, we all have to work with the material we've been given. Before he became a writer, Po Bronson shares, "I'd done nothing but haul my [butt] to work, slowly gravitating towards work that was less objectionable." Is this you? Let's direct a new course that focuses on what you're areas of strength.

What Are Your Strengths?

Need some help coming up with areas of strength? Here are some questions I ask my clients:

- What do you naturally gravitate towards?
- What compels you to action?
- What do other people say you're good at?
- If you could go back in time and change one thing about your life, what would it be?

- If you won the lottery and money wasn't an issue, what job would you pursue?
- What meaningful events or critical turning points in your life have impacted you? Why?
- Who has succeeded in the field you want to succeed in? Can you emulate them?

Even if you started with one of these questions, it could propel other thoughts and ideas that lead to further discoveries about yourself. I firmly believe that if more people took an inventory of what their true strengths and passions were, we'd have a lot less unsatisfied employees and significantly less turnover in the workplace. Over 70% of US employees are either dissatisfied or actively dissatisfied with their work and career choices. Read that again. Seven out of 10 of your co-workers are not happy with their jobs.

It's because they are not working from their strengths.

Work from Your Strengths

As I advise others to work from their strengths, I took the time to reflect on my own.

These are examples of my strengths and my thought processes as I have arrived at them:

1. I like to ask questions. I can do the small talk thing well enough, but I really like to know what makes people tick. Due to the nature of my profession, I often speak with people that are in "transition" or between jobs, or just plain unhappy with their lives. But it's only when someone is ready to pursue change that I really enjoy working with them. We become like-minded people who are energetic, enthusiastic, and excited about life. This gets me going.

2. I have a strong ability to see beyond the periphery and get to the heart of the matter. As a former IT Auditor, one of my

jobs was to see past the symptoms and get to the root cause of the issue. This has served me well as a professor, trainer, and consultant.

3. I am a non-judgmental listener that is able to hear a problem and identify opportunities for change. I can adapt within many social and corporate settings. I have worked in the corporate world for over 15 years and with my doctorate, I am able to use my analytical and logical problem-solving skills to communicate with leadership at various levels.

See, that wasn't that bad, was it? Do I come off as a self-absorbed oaf?

This exercise takes a little bit of time and introspection, but it's important for you to consider where your strengths are.

Passion Doesn't Care Where You Live

Have you ever had a friend that was passionate about something? I mean someone who lives, eats, breathes, and constantly talks about a certain thing or hobby? My friend David Altrogge is a filmmaker. He knew he wanted to be a filmmaker and producer since he was a little kid. He read books on filmmaking, video production, and creative design. His hobbies, interests, and even his college degree are aligned with pursuing his dream of being a movie producer. He always watched the special Director's Cuts versions that came with DVD packages. He is constantly reading, writing, and editing his scripts and researching how to be better at his craft.

One small problem. David grew up in a little town called Indiana, Pennsylvania. Where it's one claim to fame: it's the hometown of Jimmy Stewart (It's a Wonderful Life). Do you know how many famous movie directors have come out of Indiana, PA? Zero. David loves his hometown, he's involved with his church, married a local girl and they're raising a small family where he grew up. He's living a comfortable life, but what about his passion?

In the real world he has two options, stay in Podunk, USA and be a responsible family man and grow up, get a haircut, and a real job. Or option #2, uproot his young family to New York or Los Angeles and make the necessary sacrifices to give his dream the real opportunity it needs.

So what did David do? Neither. He made option #3. He started his own film production company in his hometown.

Based out of Indiana, PA, Vinegar Hill Creative (www.vinegarhillcreative.com) has taken David across the world to film promo spots, commercials, documentaries and even produce his own feature films. David has worked with global companies including Proctor & Gamble, Netflix, The Discovery Channel, Travel Channel, and more. He's won various awards for his work and is still constantly working on his craft. David's passion is to write and tell stories through film. He loves this creative aspect of his job. Even when filming a commercial or a promotional spot, he gets to control the flow and content of the story.

Your passion doesn't care where you live. You can be successful where you are, but it takes diligence and persistence.

David has completely devoted himself to his passion and you can tell by the quality of his work. Has he made it big? Maybe not by Hollywood standards, but his small business is growing and I have no doubt that we will see his company continue to do great things.

> **"If we did all the things we are capable of doing, we'd be astonished at what we've accomplished!"**
>
> **~Thomas Edison**

No Talent Required

You still may have some reservations in your head about pursuing your dreams, especially if you feel like you lack the necessary talent to pursue your dreams. If you only look at what you can't do, you already have a built-in excuse. So what are the things you can cultivate right now that don't require any talent?

Are you able to be more punctual for your meetings? Are you able to get up 30 minutes earlier and shorten lunch to 30 minutes and gain a whole hour of productivity, exercise, or stress management for your day?

Are you able to show respect and courtesy to others (even when you're driving)? Are you able to show kindness and mercy towards someone who is rude? These are all things that don't require much talent but lay a foundation for you to build your network and increase your influence on others.

Zappos

Zappos is a company that is obsessed with the customer. This is their entire mission statement in one phrase: Customer obsession. I love this company. I still have not bought anything from them, but I know I eventually will.

They first started as an online shoe retailer. With the cost savings of not having a brick and mortar store – they were able to pass along the savings to their customers. They provided higher quality shoes at a less than premium price. From a marketing perspective, that's a pretty good position of strength.

But here's the kicker – you can return the shoes at any point for up to one year (365 days) to receive a full refund or exchange for new shoes. They pay for shipping both ways. They have eliminated the two most common barriers to purchasing shoes online. People are worried the shoes won't fit and they don't want to pay for returning them. The inconvenience and cost of delivery and returns is assumed by Zappos at no additional cost to the customer.

Their customer service representatives are among the best in the e-commerce industry with an average of over 5 years' experience. Most CSRs have a turnover ratio of 18 months on average.

Here's another interesting strategy they employ – CSRs are encouraged to spend as much time as they need to meet their customers' needs. Contrary to most call centers, where performance is measured by how many calls are processed, Zappos does not measure the quantity of the calls.

I tested this out and called the 1-800-927-7671 toll free call center number to see if I could ask a few questions. Sandy picked up the phone and I told her from the outset that I was not interested in purchasing anything. I just wanted to learn more about the company. I kept her on as long as I could to see if she would try to end the call, but she didn't. I spoke with her for 47 minutes.

The only reason I stopped, was because I had another meeting that I had to go to or else, I'm sure we could have gone for over an hour. Am I saying Zappos takes on "No Talent" people? Of course not. Sandy probably could work anywhere, but she loves the company and has been with them for over 7 years. Does it take talent to be courteous and helpful? Not really, but Zappos has taken its mission of being customer-obsessed into billion dollar global phenomenon.

Success doesn't require talent as much as it requires persistence to do things the right way.

Am I Smart Enough?

It is a common belief that IQ (Intelligence Quotient) is a static number that is assigned and stays with you for life. Like a permanent record. But in actuality, IQ does change.

During the early 1900s, French psychologists Alfred Binet and Theodore Simon developed a series of questions that focused on testing problem-solving, attention span, and memory skills for grade-school children. This test was designed help identify which students were mostly likely to experience difficulty in schools.

Binet recognized that some younger children were able to answer more advanced questions that older children were able to answer. Based on this observation, Binet suggested the concept of a mental age, or a measure of intelligence based on the average abilities of children of a certain age group.

This first intelligence test, referred to today as the Binet-Simon Scale, became the basis for the intelligence tests still in use today. However, Binet himself did not believe his psychometric instruments could be used to measure a single, permanent and inborn level of intelligence.[2] Binet stressed the limitations of the test, suggesting that intelligence is far too broad a concept to quantify with a single number. Instead, he insisted that intelligence is influenced by a number of factors, changes over time, and can only be compared among children with similar backgrounds.[3]

Smart Enough for the Supreme Court

A recent capital punishment case within a Florida prison involved Freddie Lee Hall, a 68-year old convicted murderer on death row since 1978. Hall was convicted of murdering three people.

In Florida, as well as many other states, a capital offense can only be carried out if the convicted felon has an IQ level above 70. Basically, are you 'smart' enough to be punished for your crimes?

At the time of his arrest, Hall had an IQ of 60, however in later years his IQ was measured between 71 and 73. In a 5 to 4 ruling, the Supreme Court concluded the state's rigid IQ cutoff of 70 creates unacceptable risk that an intellectually disabled inmate might be executed in violation of the Constitution. The Supreme Court decided the convict was smart enough for his sentence to be carried out however the rigidity of the IQ number could lead to unconstitutional consequences.

Although the tale is grim, this goes to show the elasticity of our level of intelligence.

It's not a static number. In fact, the number for minimum IQ is recalibrated every 20 years to account for the overall change in mean IQ score for the population. It fluctuates and tends to ebb and flow, but the later years lead to a higher average score. So if you are planning on committing a crime, it is probably better for you to do it later rather than earlier in that 20 year cycle.

How Are You Intelligent?

How intelligent are you is a common question, but ultimately, it's the wrong one. It's not how intelligent are you, but how are you intelligent? The theory of multiple intelligences explains that intelligence can be measured in multiple ways using various metrics that include logical, mathematical, spatial, linguistic, kinesthetic, musical, and communication intelligences.

This is clear when we see professional athletes. Their physical prowess, kinesthetic dexterity, and spatial intelligence are incredible. But have you heard some of them in post-game interviews? Difficult to understand at times. If you have a minute, Google "Ryan Lochte stupid quotes." These quotes are not satire or irony. He is a world class Olympic athlete who probably won't ever be mistaken for a Rhodes Scholar.

In reality, every one possesses a unique blend of all the intelligences. Howard Gardner in his 1983 book *Frames of Mind: The Theory of Multiple Intelligences* firmly maintains that his theory should empower learners, not restrict them to one modality of learning.

According to Gardner [4], intelligence is:

1. The ability to create an effective product or offer a service that is valued in a culture.
2. A set of skills that make it possible for a person to solve problems in life.
3. The potential for finding or creating solutions for problems, which involves gathering new knowledge.

> **"If you haven't found it yet, keep looking. Don't settle. As with all matters of the heart, you'll know when you find it." ~ Steve Jobs**

Pick a Lane

Ultimately, you have to make a choice. You might be good at a lot of things, but you can't pursue two things at once. Our brains are not designed for this.

Joe Calloway, author of *Be the Best at What Matters Most*, calls it "picking a lane." You need to focus on a passion and go for it.

Don't worry if you feel like this is going to ruin your life because you picked the wrong lane. It won't. First off, you're in a lane. This is better than staying still. You're moving in a direction of a strength, interest, and passion. This is already better than what you've been doing, drifting backwards.

Second, your interests, passions, and strengths develop and change over time. Much like your multiple intelligences grow and develop, so will your dreams. What you consider a lane right now probably will look different 5 years from now. You can't control what happens 5 years from now. You can only control today. This is okay. Actually, this is better than okay. It means you've moved forward.

This is progress.

Personality Tests

Have you taken any quizzes online that tell you who you are? I see one on Facebook almost every day. Perhaps those Facebook quizzes won't be en vogue by the time you're reading this. It's the Internet; these things have a short shelf life. I'm not even sure Facebook will be around by the time you read this.

There is this growing myth that your personality type determines who you really are. So when it all comes down, you revert back to your most natural state. We are all fascinated with personality tests. No kidding, today I just saw a *'Which Sandwich Are You?'* and *'Which Disney Princess Are You?'* quizzes. Unbelievable. I'm a Reuben and Rapunzel. Who knew? See, we all want to know who we are. Most people are seeking a deeper meaning and understanding of why they do what they do.

A part of this yearning is so that we can explain what happens in our lives. This is especially true when things go wrong. In a not so subtle way, it provides a rationalization or reason for why you haven't succeeded. If you are classified as an introvert then of course you can't be successful at that sales job. If you aren't one of those creative 'artsy-fartsy' types, then of course you won't get along with the tree-hugging-hemp-wearing barista at the responsibly-grown and fair-trade-only-patchouli-smelling coffee shop. Seriously, what's with the scarf and the thin V-neck t-shirt? It's July.

Or even worse, you take one of those personality/job tests to see what type of career you should pursue. When I took that in high school I got: Policeman, Pediatrician, and High School Guidance Counselor. I can't think of three more disparate categories for a life's profession.

I ended up being none of those things. But the danger in relying on these types of assessments is that it limits your beliefs. It puts boundaries on who you are. Are you an introvert or an extravert? Are you a leader or a follower? Are you creative or do you thrive in routine? The list goes on. And once you've 'found' who you are, now you're free to go about perpetuating that stereotype.

Not Just Who but Where?

Now before you brand me a heretic, let me say that I personally have taken several personality assessments and have found most of them to be both useful and insightful. In fact, I'm going to go over the ones that I've particularly enjoyed and share my results with you. I think they can offer valuable perspectives when used as a supplement to where we are.

That's right. Where we are matters just as much as who we are. If I were to ask you what is your leadership style: 'Dominant and Assertive' or 'Collaborative and Team-Building?' How would you answer? If you think about it, it depends on the situation. It should depend on where you are in life and what circumstance you are in. Are you at the office and have 300 people reporting to you or are you at home with your three pre-teen kids?

It's called situational leadership. We are all situational leaders. We live multiple lives. We respond differently to stimuli and scenarios depending on what role we happen to be playing. Our personality types don't live in a vacuum. They live in the real world with real people and responsibilities.

Frames

My doctoral dissertation advisor, Dr. Robert Skovira defined the world by 'frames.' That is, we all have our frames we live in. We have our work frame in the office, where perhaps we are the more reserved and well-respected CFO, and then we have our home and family frame where we are the fun-loving prankster father of two young children, and then we have our hobby frame where we practice Brazilian Jiu-Jitsu and enjoy kicking a few heads in. If you were to look at the personality profile of this person, you might suggest there is a multiple-personality disorder. But it's completely normal and healthy to have the same person act and respond in different ways depending on what frame they are in.

We are a product of where we are as much as who we are.

This should be freeing. You know why? Because things change. There is fluidity to our circumstances and our surroundings. And as logical and rational beings **we need to be able to adapt to the changes around us**.

> **Fit no stereotypes. Don't chase the latest management fads. The situation dictates which approach best accomplishes the team's mission.**
>
> **~ Colin Powell**

Ambivert

Have you ever heard someone say, *"oh he's an introvert – he's just not that good with people."* Well I don't doubt that he's not that good with people in that setting, but if he has any relationships at all, I'm sure his family and friends would provide plenty of evidence that he's great with people.

Traditionally, being an extravert meant you were extremely outgoing, verbose, and comfortable in a crowd. Being an introvert meant you were extremely shy, quiet, and don't like being with other people.

But these stereotypes never worked for us.

There is no such thing as a pure introvert or extravert. Such a person would be in the lunatic asylum. ~ Carl Jung

Are there tendencies in which we naturally gravitate towards? Yes, but those aren't set in stone nor are they completely true regardless of the environment. In reality, introversion and extraversion are a range within a continuum rather than a single score on a test.

Think more along the lines of those old-time doctor's office scales with the balanced weights as opposed to one of those digital Weight Watchers scales. I hate both instruments, but just to illustrate the point there is a range of personality depending on situation as opposed to an exact number every time.

Introverts, or those who tend to lean toward that end of the scale are more likely to have their energy sapped by being in large crowds. Introverts can be energized simply sitting alone by the fire with a nice book.

Extraverts, or those who lean towards the opposite end of the continuum, gain energy and enthusiasm interacting with other people, particularly within larger crowds. Extraverts can find their energy is drained when they spend too much time alone.

For most of us, we could probably recall instances where both circumstances were true. Personally, I tend to lean towards the Extravert side of the scale, I love being around new people, ideas, and chatter. I love conference ballrooms and opening night ceremonies and all the hoopla. But I also love sitting alone and collecting my thoughts and reading a good book. There are times when I've enjoyed my time socializing with large groups of people, and then it's time to go away and be alone.

In reality, we are situational ambiverts. We're both introverted and extraverted depending on the circumstances and what our surroundings demand from us.

> **"My point is, life is about balance. The good and the bad. The highs and the lows. The pina and the colada."**
> **~ Ellen DeGeneres**

The A-Team

Naturally when you think of different personality types, we are quick to see how differently people think from us. And this can be a difficult challenge to overcome. If you normally see your way of thinking as the 'right' way, there are multiple ways in which other people could be wrong. So anyone who acts and responds differently than you is automatically wrong, and you need to convince them of how wrong they are.

This is not an effective use of your time.

Think more like Colonel John "Hannibal" Smith, the leader of the A-Team. He knew he needed a strong and diverse team to make his plans come together. So he had 'Face' to woo and subdue the female enemy combatants, 'Mad Murdock' as the crazy and fearless pilot, and 'B.A. Baracus' as the muscle and weapons guy.

Most successful business ventures were created by teams. Think of Apple's Steve Jobs, Steve Wozniak, and Ronald Wayne. Ronald Wayne? Jobs was the visionary, Woz was the engineer, and Wayne provided his personal assets as debt collateral for Apple to get initial financing. Google's Larry Page and Sergey Brin were the virtuoso programmers behind Google's algorithms but still needed Eric Schmidt to serve as CEO to properly build organizational infrastructure.

Knowing your own personality type and your team's personalities, preferences, and decision making styles can be extremely useful when working together. If you know someone who is very detail-oriented and thrives within routinized tasks, by all means let that person use their strengths and provide you with ample research data. If you have another person who is more abstract, can think outside the box, and is an idea generator, then use their natural skills and preferences in the ideation phase.

Know who's on your team and what their styles and preferences are so when the situation arrives you have a clear understanding of who you're A-Team is.

Personality Assessments

Personality assessments are exactly what they sound like. These personality tests describe and explain the characteristics and qualities of that person's particular make-up. In many ways these tests can provide a unique perspective and awareness of what makes us different.

So what are the more commonly known personality assessments?

There are numerous personality tests available, but the assessments I commonly deal with and discuss within organizations are:

1. **Meyers Briggs Type Indicator (MBTI)**
2. **The Big Five Factors**
3. **DISC Assessment**

Meyers Briggs Type Indicator (MBTI)

The MBTI assessment is a questionnaire that measures one's preferences and how they respond to different social and environmental surroundings. The crux of the MBTI is to determine how an individual usually reacts to a given scenario.

For instance one of the scenario statements on the MBTI may be:

You are easily affected by strong emotions.

Answer Options: *YES or NO*

Notice, there is no maybe, sometimes, or it depends? This is by design. The assessment is forcing you to give a binary response. The problem is your responses may or may not be true all of the time, depending on the given circumstance.

	4 Pairs of the MBTI	
#1	E = Extraversion	I = Introversion
#2	S = Sensing	N = Intuition
#3	T = Thinking	F = Feeling
#4	J = Judging	P = Perception

What's Your Score?

An example MBTI score would be **ENFP** or "**Extraversion-Intuition-Feeling-Perception.**"

Let's break it down by each of the construct pairs.

(E) Extraversion vs. (I) Introversion

Measures Attitude: What's your attitude towards interacting with others?

A preference or attitude score of E (Extraversion) means that you enjoy interacting with many people in a highly energized and enthusiastic environment as opposed to an I (Introversion) who would rather spend more quality time with one or two people. You also tend to act before you think. You are more of an action-oriented person. This energizes an E, whereas quiet and solitude energize an I.

(S) Sensing vs. (N) Intuition

Measures Information: How do you perceive and interpret new information?

A score of N (Intuition) means that you prefer to trust your gut instinct. You are more trusting of information that can be abstract or theoretical, and you are interested in how this could impact the bigger, grander picture. Someone with a score of S (Sensing) is more interested in the hard facts. They need data that is detailed, specific, and vetted. They do not go with hunches or guesses; the data is all they need.

(T) Thinking vs. (F) Feeling

Measures Decisions: How do you prefer to make decisions?

A score of F (Feeling) means that you prefer to make decisions based on subjective empathy and emotion towards a certain situation. An F tries to reach a consensus by seeing the issue from the inside and seeks to consider the needs and emotions of all stakeholders. A T (Thinking) score indicates a preference to make decisions based on a standard set of rules that remain consistent and logical.

(J) Judging vs. (P) Perceiving

Measures Structure: How do you prefer to deal with the outside world?

A score of P (Perceiving) means that you prefer to keep your options open on making decisions. You are open to new information and are willing to change your opinion if there is a change in the circumstances. The J (Judging) has a set of rules and standards to judge their outside world by and they stick to it. They are logical and have made up their minds about how things work.

The Big Five Factor Traits

Another often used personality assessment tool is call the Five Factor Model. The "Big Five" factors or Five Factor Model explains personality within five (5) broad dimensions or factors (O.C.E.A.N):

1. **Openness:** How open are you to new experiences? Are you curious and inquisitive or do you remain cautious and restrained?
    a. Openness means you have a natural curiosity, creativity and a preference for new things. It also shows a preference for variety and change as opposed to the same old routine.

2. **Conscientiousness:** How organized and prepared are you? Do you have a tendency to be organized and dependable, and show self-discipline?
    a. Conscientiousness means that you like to properly plan out your actions before pursuing them. You are

more of a rule follower as this is the correct way to do anything.

3. **Extraversion:** Are you outgoing and enthusiastic about life?
   a. Extraversion points to the need to interact and talk with others. To be actively social and to exchange new ideas, energy, and inspiration in group settings.

4. **Agreeableness:** Are you naturally friendly and amicable?
   a. Agreeableness shows a tendency to be compassionate and empathetic rather than suspicious and cold towards others. It is also a measure of one's trusting and helpful nature, and whether a person is generally well tempered or not.

5. **Neuroticism:** How emotionally stable are you? Are you easily angered or annoyed?
   a. Neuroticism means a leaning to experience unpleasant emotions easily, such as anger, anxiety, depression, and vulnerability. Essentially everyone in traffic or the DMV would show a high level of neuroticism.

These 5 Factors are scaled from 0-100%. Your results are compared to the average of all other participants and you receive a rating between 0-100 for each of the factors.

An example Big 5 Factor score could be:

> **SCORE: O (90) – C (35) – E (91) – A (79) – N (5)**

Where Can I Take the Big 5 Factor Test?

I took the 10 minute assessment here:

http://www.outofservice.com/bigfive/

Here is a deeper analysis of the Big 5 results below:

	●Your Results	
Closed-Minded	├————————●┤	Open to New Experiences
Disorganized	├——●————┤	Conscientious
Introverted	├————●┤	Extraverted
Disagreeable	├———●—┤	Agreeable
Calm / Relaxed	├●————┤	Nervous / High-Strung

What aspects of personality does this tell me about?
There has been much research on how people describe others, and five major dimensions of human personality have been found. The following dimensions with high and low scores mean the following:

Openness to Experience/Intellect
High scorers tend to be original, creative, curious, complex; Low scorers tend to be conventional, down to earth, narrow interests, uncreative.

Conscientiousness
High scorers tend to be reliable, well-organized, self-disciplined, careful; Low scorers tend to be disorganized, undependable, and negligent.

Extraversion
High scorers tend to be sociable, friendly, fun loving, talkative; Low scorers tend to be introverted, reserved, inhibited, and quiet.

Agreeableness
High scorers tend to be good natured, sympathetic, forgiving, courteous; Low scorers tend to be critical, rude, harsh, and callous.

Neuroticism
High scorers tend to be nervous, high-strung, insecure, worrying; Low scorers tend to be calm, relaxed, secure, and hardy.

What do the scores tell me?

In order to provide a meaningful comparison, the scores have been converted to "percentile scores." This means that your personality score can be directly compared to another group of people who have also taken this personality test.

The percentile scores show you where you score on the five personality dimensions relative to the comparison sample of other people who have taken this test on-line. For example, if your Extraversion percentile score is 91, this means that 91 percent of the people in our comparison sample are less extraverted than you -- in other words, you are strongly extraverted. Keep in mind that these percentile scores are relative to the study population. Thus, your percentile scores may differ if you were compared to another sample (e.g., elderly British people).

(Source: http://www.outofservice.com/bigfive/)

DISC Assessment

The DISC test is a behavior and personality style assessment tool based on the DISC theory of psychologist, Dr. William Marston. Marston's theory centers on four different personality traits:

1. **Dominance: How one approaches problems and challenges.**
    a. Individuals with a high "D" dimension tend to be bold, spirited and adventurous. These are people with a high sense of urgency, are very demanding, and are aggressive when seeking solutions to problems. High D's are direct, straight-forward, and don't mince words. They are also easily angered.

2. **Influence: How one interacts with and influences people.**

   a. Individuals with a high "I" dimension are very friendly, are able to influence others, and are usually the life of the party. They get along with everyone and they have no enemies. High I's are optimistic and the glass is always half full in almost any situation. High I's are people-oriented, enthusiastic about life and possibilities, and willing to try new ideas and rely on people and their team.

3. **Steadiness: How one responds to changes and new activities.**

   a. Individuals with a high "S" dimension are "go with the flow" people. They are easygoing and like to maintain the status quo. High S's are loyal team players that are excellent at getting their work done from start to finish. They tend to be logical thinkers and are more realistic than their dreamy counterparts. They can also seem unattached emotionally as they rely more on facts than feeling.

4. **Compliance: How one responds to rules and regulations.**

   a. Individuals with a high "C" dimension are rule followers that want to get things right the first time. They are meticulous with the details and seek quality over quantity. They prefer using highly proven methods are excellent at digging below the surface to get to the root issues.

Where Can I Take a Sample DISC Assessment?

You can take the 20 minute assessment here: http://discpersonalitytesting.com/free-disc-test/show-work-results/

A sample DISC Profile Assessment result is shown here:

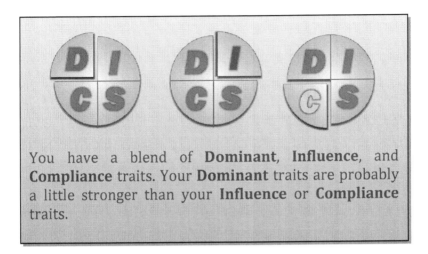

You have a blend of **Dominant**, **Influence**, and **Compliance** traits. Your **Dominant** traits are probably a little stronger than your **Influence** or **Compliance** traits.

Some words that describe you are:

- Directive,
- Quick-witted,
- Results-oriented, and fast-paced

You have both task-oriented and people-oriented traits. While you tend towards an outgoing and fast-paced approach, you can either be reserved or outgoing depending on the situation. You probably enjoy solving problems and making things happen. You are comfortable interacting with people for this purpose. You probably like to do things quickly, and you are probably comfortable working with many people in varied environments.

(Source: http://discpersonalitytesting.com/free-disc-test/show-work-results/)

A Whole New Way of Thinking

Daniel Pink in his book *A Whole New Mind* advocates a new way of thinking about personality types. Don't just hire MBA's to be managers, consider hiring poets, artists, graphic designers. We've moved from the Agriculture to the Industrial Age – and we are currently moving from the Information Age to the Conceptual Age – there is a need to recognize the power of creativity and abstraction.

While Pink does make a compelling argument for considering the power of right-brained people – he also concedes that both sides of the brain play an intricate role in everything we do. They are connected.

We're all analytical and creative in the appropriate context and environment. Regardless of what your personality assessment reports, don't limit yourself in terms of analytical versus creative.

Personality tests can be very useful when dealing with other people. You will be better prepared to deal with communication issues and conflicts when you can see things from their point of view.

Though it's not as exciting to be considered a jack of all trades, in reality this is who we are. We need balance in our lives. When the circumstances demand, we will need to be Dominant and Extraverted in our responses, whereas in other situations, it is best if we lean more towards our Conscientious and Introverted preferences.

The key to success is to understand there are multiple perspectives on personality. In certain situations you will respond differently than if you would in the exact same scenario but within a new environment.

Chapter 6 Notes:

1. Wilt Chamberlain still holds the record with 5,805 missed free throws. *Way to go Wilt!*
2. Kamin, L. J. (1995). The pioneers of IQ testing. In Ressell Jacoby & Naomi Glauberman (Eds.), The Bell Curve Debate: History, Documents, Opinions. New York: Times Books.
3. Siegler, R. S. (1992). The other Alfred Binet. *Developmental Psychology, 28,* 179-190.
4. Howard Gardner in his 1983 book *Frames of Mind: The Theory of Multiple Intelligence.*

> "You can't connect the dots looking forward; you can only connect them looking backwards. So you have to trust that the dots will somehow connect in your future."
>
> ~ Steve Jobs

Chapter 7: Connect the Dots

I have this phrase on my vision board that says, "Inspiration happens everywhere."

The reason we lose sight of inspiration is because life happens everywhere too. And for most people life is simply getting through the drudgery of the week so you can do what you want on the weekend. Life can also become discouraging when you try to make changes and you see no outcomes. It's tough to keep trying to change and improve when you get no results.

Find Your Groove

One of the primary steps to achieving success, specifically within your career is to find out what has worked for you in the past. Often we're so enamored with what's currently popular that we don't appreciate what we've been able to accomplish thus far.

Maybe you're a musician and you're good with people, and you love animals. Or perhaps in your previous job you were the best researcher and your teachers have consistently lauded you as a talented writer. For others it may be more difficult to pinpoint where your talents are. This was the case for me a few years back.

Career Arc Timeline

I was at the National Speaker's Annual Convention a few years ago and a well-known speaker and friend by the name of Glenna Salsbury asked me one time, *what are you passionate about?* I said, *I'm not sure* – but there are a lot of things that I like and don't like. Then she said, *well what do other people say you're good at?* I responded as honestly as I could, but it was a hodge-podge of different skills and talents.

One of the recommendations she gave was to draw a career arc timeline. List all of the jobs and places you've worked. This will map out the what, where, and who you've been in your career up to this point. Glenna went on to explain that you'll most likely see some common themes or motifs that pop up from your previous life and career choices. So even if they don't align with your hobbies or interests right now, there are going to be themes and topics that emerge from your career.

It was a pretty eye-opening experience. I recommend you try this same exercise.

Here's how to create a Career Arc Timeline:

1. List all of the jobs you've ever had. Think as far back as you can remember. While it doesn't have to be in a particular order, I found it helpful to work backwards (most recent jobs first).
   a. Here are a sample of my **current and previous jobs**:
      i. **Professor of Business** (2010 – Present)
      ii. **VP Information Security** (2007 – 2010)
      iii. **IT Auditor** (2000 – 2007)
      iv. Etc.

2. List some of the <u>key responsibilities and duties</u> you performed while working at these jobs.
    a. Here are my **Key Duties and Responsibilities**:
        i. Professor of Business (2010 – Present)
            1. **Teaching**
            2. **Advising**
            3. **Research**
        ii. VP Information Security (2007 – 2010)
            1. **Managed information security infrastructure**
            2. **Investigated security breaches and threats**
            3. **Implemented various info sec policies**
        iii. Etc.

3. What are some of the <u>key common themes or characteristics</u> that come up from each of the jobs?
    a. Here are my **Key Themes/Characteristics**:
        i. Professor of Business (2010 – Present)
            1. Teaching
                a. **Highly interactive**
                b. **Very social**
                c. **Presentation skills**
                d. **Public speaking**
                e. **Utilizing technology**
            2. Advising
                a. **Coaching and mentoring**
                b. **Speaking with people and getting to the root of the issue.**
            3. Research
                a. **Look for the facts before making a decision**

b. **Asking tons of questions**

c. **Creative problem solving**

d. **Problem identification**

e. **Managing projects, timelines, and budgets**

List all of the common themes found in your entire career arc. Translate those themes into short action sentences or phrases. See my examples below. You're going to have more than 10 themes, but pick and rank your top 10 themes.

b. Here are my **Top 10 Key Themes**:

1:	Influencing, leading, and persuading others
2:	High level of interaction with other people
3:	Helping others achieve their goals
4:	Learning new material and expanding resource base
5:	Creative approaches to problem solving
6:	Speaking and presenting skills
7:	Coaching, advising, and mentoring
8:	Using resources that are currently available
9:	Utilizing and leveraging technology
10:	Manage risk prior to decision-making

What Does This Mean?

After you've identified your own themes, review them again. See if they truly match who you are.

If these 10 Themes resonate with who you are and how you live your life, this is good – you now have a clearer view of what is important to you. These are the themes and life habits that are natural to you regardless of vocation.

If your current career goals do not reflect these themes, then you should consider where you can best utilize these natural talents and habits.

Keep in mind, your current job may not directly relate to all of these themes, but it's helpful to know what specific areas you excel in and what you value. Even if these themes and topics aren't a part of your job description today, could you implement them into your work somehow?

You can be a leader, even when you aren't being paid for it. You can serve, coach, and mentor other colleagues by helping them reach their full potential. In fact, most of these actions and habits will lead to higher engagement in your workplace and increased personal satisfaction.

For me this was a revelation. I realized my talents and interests were in alignment with what I am currently doing. I am a professor, consultant, author, and professional speaker.

I love the opportunity to speak in front of people because I really like people. I like teaching them new ideas and techniques that might make their lives easier or more effective. I enjoy the high level of interaction with my clients, students, and training participants. I enjoy learning and researching new ideas, technologies, and strategies and I love that my work helps others achieve their goals.

Observe Your Environment

Dr. Amy Baxter, a pediatrician, was struggling with an effective way to administer injections for her pediatric patients without causing any additional undue trauma. Not only were her patients already in pain, but the children had to endure the anticipation of further pain with the dreaded needle. Needlephobia is alive and well among all ages, but especially young children.

Pain is more than just the actual physical act; it is compounded by the fear of the pain as well as how much attention is given to the pain. Pain can be mitigated by Gate Control Theory, which states that if you can block the small and large nerve fibers from sending the pain message to the brain, essentially "closing the gate" to the spinal cord, you can reduce pain.

As Dr. Baxter was driving home after a long shift, she noticed her hands became numb at the steering wheel. Moreover, as she thought about her problem, she knew cold packs and compresses reduced pain and inflammation to injured areas. Finally she thought about her own son who also suffered from needlephobia. As a mother, she remembered having to use various distractions for her children before giving them their shots.

Buzzy® is Born

There were three dots that needed to be connected.

1. Vibration (hands numb on the steering wheel)
2. Cold (ice packs for inflammation)
3. Distraction (Dr. Baxter's young son's toys)

Buzzy® is born. Buzzy is a tiny, vibrating ice pack in the shape of a toy bumblebee used to help ease pain from injections and infusions for pediatric patients. With a solid idea, Dr. Baxter was able to secure over $1.1M in grant funding and several other doctors, attorneys, and MBAs joined her team to create and build her business.

Today, over 1200 hospitals and more than 36,000 users have adopted Buzzy®. Buzzy® was a 2011 Medical Design Excellence Awards recipient and Top 10 Innovative Technology Company in 2012.

Pay attention to your surroundings.

Observe your environment. Connect the dots.

> **"Take time to gather up the past so that you will be able to draw from your experience and invest them in the future."**
>
> **~Jim Rohn**

> **"Remember kids, the only difference between screwing around and science is writing stuff down."**
>
> **~ Adam Savage (Mythbusters)**

Chapter 8: Write Stuff Down

Because We Forget Stuff

I have had the privilege of presenting at and attending over 100 academic and industry conferences. And of those 100+ conferences and webinars, in the past 15 years, I've had the opportunity of sitting in over 1000 presentations. When I review all of the notes I've taken while listening to each presenter, I am amazed at how much I've forgotten.

The notes are in my handwriting or on my smartphone, so I know I was there. I was cognizant enough to pay attention and write the notes that I found to be useful and helpful, and yet re-reading some of these annotations is like finding a treasure all over again. It's so easy to forget stuff. You know you're not going to remember this later without jotting down a note, so do yourself a favor – alleviate the stress and frustration of not being able to recall information and write it down.

Another benefit of writing down notes is you may find a certain nugget of truth wasn't applicable to you then, but it is now. Or it may be useful in the future. It's a life truth: when the student is ready, the teacher appears.

One key element is you must actually review what you've written. If you don't, then it's almost like you never wrote it down.

I'm all for mobile apps and being able to speak your notes verbally, but there is something even more beneficial to the physical connection of putting pen to paper. It frees your mind. You can do a brain dump of everything you need to do that day without worrying about mistyping, battery life, or lack of Internet connectivity.

Ever have that great invention idea or the script for the next great American novel in your head only to have it evaporate like the morning mist? Yeah, me neither. Who knows what gems or brilliant ideas we've lost due to not writing them down?

> **"Write down the thoughts of the moment. Those that come unsought for are commonly the most valuable."**
>
> **~ Francis Bacon, Sr.**

Prioritize Your To Do List

Writing stuff down allows you to prioritize your day.

To Do Lists. I love them.

TO DO LIST

- [ ]
- [ ]
- [ ]
- [ ]
- [ ]

Do you have a To Do List?

They are a simple way to keep organized, and you don't need a fancy-shmancy app or spreadsheet. A simple blank piece of paper or sticky note will do.

Here's the process:

Write out what you want to get done for the day. You can also plan these the night before, but sometimes I have things that I need to take care of that come up on the way to work.

Write out the top 5 things you need to get done today. Prioritize the list from most important first.

How do you prioritize?

There is a simple but powerful method of ranking your To Do List. It's called **pairwise ranking method**.

List all of your priorities in a list. No need to rank them in any order. Start with To Do item #1. Pair this with To Do item #2. Which is more important? Whichever is more important moves on to the next pairwise ranking. Like the NCAA basketball tournament. You win, you move on to the next round of competition.

See the pairwise ranking example below:

To Do List:

1	Make more money
2	Write book
3	Exercise more
4	Lose weight

Pairwise ROUND 1:	Comparisons
First -	**More Important?**
# 1 vs. # 2	#1
Next -	**More Important?**
# 1 vs. # 3	#1
Next -	**Winner?**
# 1 vs. # 4	**#1**

To Do Item #1 is clearly the winner compared to all of the other items, but what about the other items on your list?

Pairwise ROUND 2:	Comparisons
First -	**More Important?**
# 2 vs. # 3	#3
Next -	**Winner?**
# 3 vs. # 4	**#4****

Now your To Do List is ranked in priority order.

**To Do Item # 4 is already ranked higher than # 2, because # 3 was already more important than # 2. Makes sense right? Try it on your own a few times, you'll get it.

Your new revised To Do List in ranking order is: #1, #4, #3, and #2.

> **To Do List:**
>
> 1 Make more money (#1)
> 2 Lose weight (#4)
> 3 Exercise more (#3)
> 4 Write book (#2)

Here's the real secret: Don't move on to #2 on your list <u>UNTIL</u> #1 is done. Don't jump around your list. Finish one task, before moving onto the next one.

This forces you to grasp what you need to get done for that day.

By default you get the important stuff done first. It's not the easiest thing to do, but remain disciplined. <u>Don't advance on your To Do List until you complete the first item.</u>

Try this for a week and see how your productivity levels increase.

It Keeps You Accountable

Writing down your goals is one of the most significant methods to achieving them. It's one thing to think you're going to lose weight and make more money. It's entirely different to write down your specific goals on paper and see them.

As an example, here are my goals for (September 2014):

1. Lose 10 lbs. in the next 2 months (November 2014).
2. Finish writing the outline for my next book in the next 3 months (December 2014).

Write your goals and place them somewhere you can see it every day.

If you're adventurous, get an accountability partner and share your goals with each other. Or start a Mastermind or Accountability group.

If you really want to get stuff done, share your goals publicly. Put these goals online and on your social media platform. Then update your tribe every week on your progress – both good and bad.

Dr. Gail Matthews' Five Groups

A study conducted by Dr. Gail Matthews, a Psychology professor at the Dominican University of California shows the power of writing down goals.

The study on goal setting was conducted with five groups.

Group 1 was asked to think about the business-related goals they hoped to accomplish within a four-week block and to rate each goal according to difficulty, importance, the extent to which they had the skills and resources to accomplish the goal.

Groups 2-5 were asked to write their goals and then rate them on the same dimensions as given to Group 1.

Group 3 was also asked to write action commitments for each goal.

Group 4 had to both write goals and action commitments and also share these commitments with a friend.

Group 5 went the furthest by doing all of the above plus sending a weekly progress report to a friend.

At the end of the study, the individuals in Group 1 only accomplished 43 percent of their stated goals. Those in Group 4 accomplished 64 percent of their stated goals, while those in Group 5 were the most successful, with an average 76 percent of their goals accomplished.

> "My study provides empirical evidence for the effectiveness of three coaching tools: accountability, commitment, and writing down one's goals" ~ Gail Matthews

It Reduces Stress

Time management expert, David Allen recommends placing your to do list and priority items into "buckets." These buckets are solely based on the ability to get things done within a strict time limit. So for instance, if the action item takes less than 2 minutes to do (e.g. write a thank you email reply, confirm a reservation, re-tweet an article) then do it right then and there. I'm not against this as I believe our lives are filled with more than just big projects and mission-critical items. But the bigger takeaway for me is that writing down your goals *can actually alleviate stress in your brain.*

When there is a project that needs our attention and we do nothing with it, it actually creates stress. Every time you see the unfinished project your mind says, *"oh darn, I really need to get that done."* But there is no time limit on this project so it creates a base level of anxiety, guilt, and concern for that unfinished task.

A simple but powerful way to relieve this stress is to write the objective down.

Because once you write it down, you are forced to place that action into a time bucket. Even when you have no real intention of finishing that item, your brain can now move on to other things. In this case you now have a "Complete When I Have Time and Really Want To" bucket.

That's it. You're free to work on other more pressing items because your brain re-categorizes the unfinished task as something you will take care of later. No need to worry about it or try to figure out where you're going to fit that into your schedule. And your guilt is assuaged because you have not ignored it.

Track Your Progress

Much like a journal, writing your goals down provides a way for you to track how you're doing. It also creates a knowledge base of previous goals, actions, and status updates. You can view this as a way to track how far you've come. It provides a way to clearly identify what areas you were able to get done and what goals you've missed.

Just like any other knowledge repository, you can use this valuable information to either spur you on to continue or to change your methods or techniques to something that was more effective. Again, we forget the great stuff we've done in the past.

Writing things down helps you gain a sense of achievement and progress, expanding your confidence.

Write Every Day

Write every day. It takes discipline, but it's worth it.

A friend of mine is a retired executive and author of 6 books (as of this writing – he may be on his 7th or 8th book by now). His name is Mike Johnson. His primary passion is writing historical fiction.

Mike was 60 years old when he wrote his first book. It took him over 2 years to write it, but he says, "it was worth every minute." After that first book, he was able to complete another historical fiction novel every year for the next 5 years. Keep in mind, these are big books, we're talking 500+ pages. What's his secret?

He writes every day. Even if it's just for a little bit, he will take time out of his day to write. It's important to be committed to the process. There is benefit to writing everyday beyond just having something to show for it. It creates a mental momentum that spurs even more writing. Writing your thoughts on a daily basis forces your brain to get beyond the surface level and down to subconscious thinking. This is where the creative magic is. But it only comes when you practice writing as a daily discipline.

I have a blog: http://write15minutes.com.

This is my secret garden where I post my thoughts on writing, productivity, and inspirational quotes. And while I try to post on the blog once a week, it's more of a reminder for me to keep writing. Even if I'm not posting daily – I still try to write every day.

Write for 15 minutes a day. Try it. Do this for a week and see what you get done.

Makes You More Effective

I realize for most jobs, you won't be required to write a book or a dissertation to complete your job responsibilities. And thank God for that. I went through it once, and I'd rather not do it again.

But in reality we're surrounded by written words. Whether it's a financial statement, audit findings, sales document, or a TPS report – you need to be able to read and write in order to do your job effectively. And as you move up the corporate ladder and gain more leadership responsibilities, your ability to communicate effectively becomes paramount. Writing daily helps you become a better communicator.

Have you had to give a keynote speech or a sales presentation to your clients or senior management? Do you realize how many people go up to the podium and just wing it? You'd be surprised. That's why our board meetings and consulting presentations are so dry and boring. People don't spend enough time writing out their speeches or presentations.

Try this the next time you're asked to give a speech. Write down your script as if you're going to be on TV. This will sharpen your focus. You will be less inclined to rely on filler words like *uh, um,* and *like*. You will know exactly where your speech or presentation is going because you've written it out and planned ahead. Rather than seeming stuffy and rehearsed, this actually gives you the freedom to improvise and adjust as you see fit. Most importantly, you are able to communicate your message without wasting your audience's time.

Chapter 8 Notes:

1. Dr. Gail Matthews – Five Groups Study
   http://www.dominican.edu/dominicannews/study-backs-up-strategies-for-achieving-goals
2. David Allen – Getting Things Done
   http://gettingthingsdone.com/

> "Everyone needs deadlines."
>
> ~ Walt Disney

Chapter 9: Mini-Project Manager

Everything's a project. As I was looking over my past year, the goals I was able to accomplish were either big projects or a series of separate mini-projects. Then it hit me, *we're all Mini-Project Managers.*

To provide a little context, some of my goals this past year included: complete my online social media course development, submit and present at various conferences, develop an outline for my book, and paint the back deck. There was some overlap and integration among the various responsibilities, but overall most of the items were fairly big projects that had a definite goal and due date. Of course I had other duties and tasks for my profession, but these are the projects that had a definite end date.

For most people, the work you do will be a mixture of three different responsibilities:

1. **Daily Routine Activities**
2. **Maintenance Activities**
3. **Mini-Projects**

Daily routines are fairly self-explanatory. These are the daily routinized tasks that you are able to do without much thought. Cleaning out your email inbox, checking your work schedule for the day, turning on the printer, fax machine, logging into multiple systems, and checking the status of your work.

Maintenance activities involve a little more thought. These could be any types of upkeep, quick fixes, or troubleshooting that needs to happen for your life to run smoothly. Perhaps there is a client complaint issue that needs to be resolved more tactfully than sending a rubber stamped email reply. There could be an issue with the new CRM system that requires some deeper digging in to find the solution.   These aren't anything new; they are maintenance activities to keep the status quo.

The last and most impactful activities are the projects. These are the projects that have a clear purpose and design to either introduce a new idea or drastically improve an old one. Projects must have a definite finish line. If you look at all of the huge projects you have yet to start, this can become daunting.   Start breaking down the project into mini-projects.

Most important tasks should be conducted this way. Whether you are working on a huge multi-stakeholder project for work or a small DIY job at home – project management principles will help you get the project completed on time within your projected scope and budget.

What is Project Management?

According to the Project Management Institute (PMI), project management can be summarized into 5 steps:

1. Initiation
2. Planning
3. Execution
4. Monitoring & Control
5. Closing

Don't Get Stuck

If you are 'think before you leap' person, you will spend most of your time in steps #1 and #2 (Initiation and Planning) and you need a gentle push to get your project started. Consider this your push. You've planned and thought out enough. Get started on your new goals.

If you are an 'action junky,' you are constantly in steps #3 and #4 (Execution and Monitoring & Control). Things get started, but they are inefficient and it takes longer to get done because you are constantly reassessing what your priorities are. There will be some benefit in soliciting and getting feedback on the initiation and planning stages. This could save you some time and future headaches by eliminating some unforeseen obstacles to your goals. This is your chance to pull back the reigns and bring in some other perspectives to get a clearer picture of the end goal.

Have a Deadline

This is the most important aspect of project management. All projects must have an end date. You need to establish a definitive date by which the project is considered complete and closed. Think of all your projects with a definite end date. This will help motivate you to get done as quickly as you can while still maintaining quality. What long-term goal or purpose will this mini-project serve?

Projects require you to take full ownership from start to end. There is no one else to blame anymore. This adds a little pressure, but you need to trust your ability to get it done. Preferably all projects would be under-budget and completed before the deadline, but like my dissertation advisor once said, a good dissertation is a done dissertation.

More than Just Showing Up

I've had students come in to my class and expect an A for just showing up. It's absolutely true that you do need to show up. This is just the bare minimum. Within a global market and increasing competition, it's no longer just enough just the show up.

To reach your goals and be successful, you need to have a plan. A plan is treating your dreams like they're worth something.

Every time you start or work on an ongoing project you are expending your time, energy, and resources to finishing this thing. The dreams and goals must be worth your time or it's not going to hold your interest.

Go Back in Time to the Future

Have you ever worked backwards? It's a fun way to get you motivated to finish your projects. Start with the end in mind with a question like – what does success look like? In other words what do you want to have done? What does a completed project look like? Now imagine you've actually completed it. It's done. Finished. It's exactly the way you envisioned this project to be. No more work on this thing.

Now use your imagination and sense of a timeline to figure out how you got here. Go back in time. What tools did you use? What did you have to do to complete this wonderful project by this date?

What mini-projects did you have to complete for this thing to come together? What milestone dates did you set for yourself to make sure you were on the right track? Which accountability partners or collaborators did you reach out to for help, editing, or review?

Now map that process out and list all of your mini-project components (start date, WBS, milestones, stakeholders, etc.). This is your master mini-project plan.

You just went back in time to re-create a future project that hasn't even started yet. Nice going. Very meta.

Removes Emotion

Treating goals like mini-projects removes emotion. You don't get too low when things don't go the way they're supposed to because you have a plan and you can adjust. You don't get too high when things get finished sooner, because you prepare for the worst, but hope for the best.

It also removes the tendency to blame. You have a plan and you should have an idea of when something is going to be done and by whom. To carry the illustration further, as the project progresses, you realize early on that a project milestone is not going to be achieved. Because you are able to catch it fairly early in the process, you know what else needs to be adjusted, changed, or removed from your project list in order for this mini-project to be completed.

Triple Constraint – Time, Scope, and Cost

Nearly anyone familiar with project management has probably heard of the famous "Triple Constraint."

Referring to the diagram above, the Triple Constraint basically demonstrates the main elements that must be handled effectively for successful completion and close of all projects.

Triple Constraints Still Apply

1. **Time** – How long will it take to produce your deliverable? Naturally, the amount of time required to produce the deliverable will be directly related to the amount of requirements that are part of the end result (scope) along with the amount of resources allocated to the project (cost).
2. **Scope** – What needs to be included in this project for this to work? What level of quality needs to be achieved for this project to be deemed a success?
3. **Cost** – How much will this cost? How many other resources (people, skills, consultants, materials, etc.) will be needed to finish this project successfully?

The Butterfly Effect

The main point of the Triple Constraint, is that one cannot adjust or modify one side of it without in effect, altering the other sides. So for example, if there is a request for a scope change mid-way through the project, the other two elements (cost and time) will be affected. How much or how little is dictated by the nature and complexity of the scope change. If the schedule appears to be tight and the scoped requirements cannot be accomplished within the allotted time, both cost and time are going to be significantly affected.

Similar to the butterfly effect, there is a risk of unknown consequences when changing one small component of a bigger ecosystem.

The mini-project manager must be fully cognizant of Time, Scope, and Cost as fully inter-related parts of a whole.

Accountability

Along with recognizing project management fundamentals, it is imperative that the mini-project manager communicates adequately to the project stakeholders. Even if you are a mini-project team of one, you should still consider involving other stakeholders to help you with ideas, knowledge, and techniques that may save you time and effort in the long run.

If you do rely on others to help you complete your mini-projects, then all the more reason to explicitly communicate what your expectations are. This creates a sense of mutual accountability. Those that agree to the scope, time, and cost are now able to help you keep track of those attributes by reporting their developments and challenges.

Even though I'm an author of one – I have outsourced some of the creative design (book cover, formatting, editing) to other people. It is my responsibility to manage those relationships and make sure I'm on schedule.

If you can perform all of these steps immediately, that's great. However, even if you start with just a few, you will have a greater control on the millions of ideas that are swimming in your head. The key is to make sure you have as much control of your mini-projects as possible. Even mini-projects can succumb to scope creep and time and cost limitations. Take control of your life and treat everything like a mini-project.

Conduct Your Own Autopsy

As painful as this is, don't let your mistakes go to waste. With every project, there should be a post-implementation review. There will always be learning opportunities if you are looking for them. Take the time to review the good, the bad, and the *really* bad.

Like a coroner that has to review all possible causes of death, have your own post-mortem review. Do this while the memories are still fairly fresh in your mind. Especially with mini-projects where you are the primary stakeholder.

Do a brain dump of all your observations. It doesn't have to be complicated. It has to be useful.

Note what worked and what didn't work. Remember to date your observations and then move on. Don't dwell on the past glories or gores of finished projects. A good project is a done project.

Chapter 9 Notes:

1. The Project Management Institute – Triple Constraints.
   http://www.pmi.org/Knowledge-Center/Next-Level-Up-
   How-Do-You-Measure-Project-Success.aspx.

> "The moment you doubt whether you can fly, you cease for ever to be able to do it."
>
> ~ J.M. Barrie, Peter Pan

Chapter 10: Inside Game

The Power of Confidence

Have you ever listened to a person who exudes confidence? I'm not talking about an ego maniac who thinks the world revolves them, I mean someone who speaks with authority and has captivating self-assurance. We are drawn to people with self-confidence. They are easy to listen to. We're more likely to follow them. It eases our anxiety on whether this person is worth our valuable time and energy. It validates our choice to listen to them.

Imagine a heart surgeon who is constantly fidgeting, appears unsure, and is noticeably nervous around people. Without saying a word, this doctor has communicated to you. How confident would you be that you're getting the best care?

Leaders must have confidence.

> "Confidence is contagious. So is lack of confidence."
> ~Vince Lombardi

Improves Performance

Noted psychologist Albert Bandura explains in his Social Cognitive Theory[1] that high level of self-efficacy (the belief that one can accomplish a task) plays a large role in determining whether you seek to master difficult task or simply avoid it.

Belief in the ability to do something makes it much more likely to get done.

Confidence can actually change your level of performance. Consider when you're learning a new skill, like riding a bicycle.

My two boys learned how to ride a bike at a young age. Were there bumps and bruises along the way? Yep. It's a rite of passage most of us have gone through. My older son Benjamin learned to ride a bike without training wheels when he was 6 years old. It took him about 6 weeks to feel fully comfortable. Sammy, his younger brother learned to ride without training wheels when he was 5 years old. He was a year younger than Benjamin when he first tried riding, but it didn't stop him. In fact, he learned how to ride his bike in <u>less than a week</u>.

They both had the same instructor (me). Both learned on the same bike. Benjamin *thought he could do it*, but Sammy *knew he could do it*. Sammy's confidence was much higher because he had the benefit of seeing his older brother do it first. His belief in his own abilities reduced his learning curve from *over a month down to one week*.

Change Your Perception, Change Your Reality

Fast forward to the summer of 2013, I was in Rome, Italy for 8 weeks teaching at our sister campus in Castel Gandolfo. I had 11 students with me. On our schedule was a three hour bike tour along the Appian Way from Rome to Lake Albano. There was one student who was reluctant to participate because she had never learned how to ride a bike. But more importantly, she did not want to learn. She lacked the belief that she could learn this new skill within the 8 weeks we were in Rome, so she decided it wasn't worth the effort.

In reality, we probably could have taught her how to ride within two weeks max, but she was not confident in her abilities or ours to teach her. It wasn't a lack of skill. Almost any able-bodied adult can learn to ride a bike. It was a lack of confidence. It was the perception that she couldn't do it and that we couldn't teach her in that short period of time.

Confidence gives you the freedom to try new things. You persevere longer because you believe actions will pay off in the long run. What you believe about yourself will change your reality.

> **"If you hear a voice within you say 'you cannot paint,' then by all means paint, and that voice will be silenced."**
> **~Vincent Van Gogh**

Time for a Little Introspection

I think introspection gets a bad rap. It can often be confused with 'navel gazing,' which is an unhealthy and limiting view of yourself and your problems. Introspection on the other hand is a more effective and useful self-examination of your thoughts and progress.

We all need a little time for self-reflection every day.

As an extravert with a high social and interactive preference, even I would go crazy if I didn't have some quality time to gather my thoughts and reflect on the day. This quiet time provides a respite from the hectic pace of the day. You are more likely to assess what progress you've made towards your goals and what areas need more attention. You can analyze past mistakes and adjust accordingly.

The Jerk Store Called

One of my favorite Seinfeld episodes is the *Comeback* where George Costanza gets burned by one of his co-workers at lunch. George is eating a huge plate of shrimp cocktail at the lunch table when he hears a jeer, *"Hey George, the ocean called, they're running out of shrimp."* George is completely embarrassed and at a loss for words because he has no comeback. As he's driving home, he finally thinks of one but it's too late.

He runs his comeback line by Jerry, Elaine, and Kramer – *"The Jerk Store called, and it's running out of you."* No one likes it and they offer their own, but George is committed to this phrase. By the end of the episode, George is finally able to use his *Jerk Store* line only to be stifled with a better response, *"What's the difference, you're their all-time best-seller."* Boom. Game, set, match. George yet again, has no response but now he's desperate. George defames the reputation of the antagonist's wife and he finally thinks he's won the battle, only to find out she's in a coma and it brings the entire mood of the office to a crawl.

Think Before You Speak

What you say matters. Obviously, you shouldn't get into shouting matches with your co-workers, but take some time to actually think about what you're going to say. Are you going into a sales pitch meeting with no idea what to say?

Do you practice role plays or scenarios before you conduct a sales call? Envision how you're going to broach the subject. Imagine what their response is going to be. What are the possible objections to your idea? What are the potential comebacks or responses that will carry the conversation? What are the key points you want to stick to?

I think we should ban all tweets for professional athletes, actors, and the Kardashians (are they still around?). In the hyper-connected world of social media, we really need some <u>time to think before we hit send</u>. Have you ever regretted sending an angry email or Facebook post? It feels horrible. It makes you look bad. Because then you either have to publicly apologize or dig your heels in further to justify your stance.

The best thing to do is to take a moment or a few moments to think before you reply. If you do happen to make a regrettable post or email reply, then make it right by apologizing and moving on.

You can even say, *"I apologize for the last post/email/reply, I clearly did not take the time to think or fully consider what my response should be. I will refrain from speaking on this subject until I can offer something of value."*

Secure Your Mask on First

I hear this every time I fly:

> "In the event of a decompression, an oxygen mask will automatically appear in front of you. To start the flow of oxygen, pull the mask towards you. Place it firmly over your nose and mouth, secure the elastic band behind your head, and breathe normally. If you are travelling with a child or someone who requires assistance, **secure your mask on first, and then assist the other person**." (Emphasis mine.)

You know the first thought that comes into my mind? *Flight attendants are selfish.* Not really. The first thought I have is, *I pray that it never happens,* but the second thought is *remember to secure my mask on first.*

You know why they say this?

In the event of cabin decompression, the oxygen levels drop drastically and you can lose consciousness quickly. You will be of no help to anyone else if you are passed out. The same is true of life. In order to best take care of your dream, family, or business – you need to take care of yourself first. This is not being selfish, this is <u>putting yourself in the best position to achieve more success</u>.

What are the things you need to change about yourself before you help others change? As a leader this will be a significant measure to live by. Do you practice what you preach? Or as we say in the consulting world, *do you eat your own dog food*?

If you value the importance of education for your employees, then how diligent are you in pursuing your own learning and growth? How many books are in your library? How many have you *actually read*?

Feeling Lucky?

Do you consider yourself lucky? Do you notice how some people tend to live a charmed life? They choose the right lane in traffic (*I hate that*). They catch the foul ball. They find loose change on the sidewalk. My younger son, Sammy is like this. He just finds treasures everywhere. If there is a contest, I'm more surprised if he doesn't win.

Psychologist, Richard Wiseman has spent years researching luck and serendipity. His research seeks to find out why some people seemed to always be in the right place at the right time.

In one experiment, he asked volunteers to read a newspaper and tell him how many photographs were inside. He also surveyed the volunteers to determine their level of serendipity. In other words, how lucky does one feel?

The two groups were then tasked with finding the total number of photos in the paper. What they didn't know was he had placed a half-page ad on the 2nd page of the newspaper that read *"Stop counting — there are 43 photographs in this newspaper."* Those who considered themselves lucky were twice as more likely to stop reading after the 2nd page.

Luck is more than just what's happening to you on the outside. It's an inside game. It's a mental view that the world is filled with various events that could lead to your benefit. Wiseman ultimately found that people are not luckier they are just quicker to spot and seize opportunities. "It was staring everyone in the face, but the unlucky people tended to miss it and the lucky people spotted it," says Wiseman. The study went on to find that people who considered themselves 'lucky' also reported higher levels of job and family satisfaction. Even though when comparing actual life circumstances, there was no difference between the two groups – luckier people are happier.

Are chance encounters an opportunity for you to develop and grow or are they nuisances to your already busy schedule? Decide to be lucky. It opens up your world to new ventures. This is like self-efficacy on overdrive. Not only are you confident in your ability to accomplish tasks, but you also *believe that the universe bends itself to offer new and exciting opportunities.*

> **I've found that luck is quite predictable. If you want more luck, take more chances. Be more active. Show up more often. ~ Brian Tracy**

Complaining Makes You Fat

What if I told you that people who complain on a consistent basis are more inclined to have poor health and tend to have lower levels of satisfaction in their relationships as well as their jobs.

It's crazy, but true. Here's why: constant complaining actually increases your cortisol levels which impacts your metabolism and immune system. This means that when you complain about being sick, tired, and gaining extra weight – you actually increase your likelihood of achieving those very outcomes.

This is a tough cycle to escape because it's self-perpetuating. Similar to the vicious cycle previously mentioned, your negative experiences feed your negative expectations, which then attract new negative experiences.

What you believe about yourself will determine how you act.

Your inside game is more about your own self-perceptions rather than how others see you.

> **"Believe in yourself! Have faith in your abilities! Without a humble but reasonable confidence in your own powers you cannot be successful or happy."**
>
> **~ Norman Vincent Peale**

Don't compare yourself to others.

You are uniquely gifted and your level of success is directly correlated to your own level of drive and determination. No one can live your life for you, and you should not try to measure your life by any standards but your own. Trust yourself enough to know what type of progress you need to be making right now.

Confidence is a choice.

You can either choose to live with confidence or insecurity. So why not choose confidence? Pursue your goals and dreams with self-assurance and poise.

Born to Win

One of my favorite speakers is Zig Ziglar. His quotes and insights have a way of inspiring me like few others do. I conclude with his encouragement and quote that we are all born to win.

> **"You were born to win, but to be the winner you were born to be you must *plan to win* and *prepare to win*!**
> **Then, and only then, can you legitimately *expect to win*."**
>
> **~Zig Ziglar**

Consider the fact that out of billions of possibilities for you NOT to be born, you somehow made it. There were many obstacles you had to overcome that were not even in your control for you to be conceived.

You competed against 300 – 400 million other cells that were racing against time and obstacles to reach a specific destination. From there, you somehow survived about 40 weeks in a womb, endured birth, made it through middle school (*this alone deserve an award*), and are now a living breathing adult human being.

Identify yourself with a positive mental image. The fact that you were born is literally a miracle against astronomical odds. You were born to win.

Chapter 10 Notes:

1. Richard Wiseman – The Luck Factor.
   http://www.richardwiseman.com/resources/The_Luck_Fa
   ctor.pdf.

"The way to get started is to quit talking and begin doing."

~Walt Disney

Conclusion: Stay the Course

Here you are. You've made it this far and finished the book. Or maybe you're like my students and you just skipped to the back of the book.

Either way, you've now reached the end of this book. You have some incredible opportunities for success in front of you. Remember the power of small wins. Don't be afraid to start small. Figure out your small doable action chunks. Rather than trying to multi-task, try compartmentalizing. Separate the multiple tasks on your list, prioritize them, and get those small wins.

Don't Be Too Busy

One word of caution: Don't mistake busy activity with actually getting things done. Is some activity better than no activity? Of course. But at a certain point, you are going to have to have a laser focus on one meaningful goal.

Full Circle

I wish I could say right after my life-changing pivot moment with my dad 20 years ago – everything changed and I became an immediate success.

Hardly.

As I entered college my freshman year, I was overwhelmed. I was completely unprepared for the amount of freedom, lack of supervision, and still had a complete disregard for the value of a formal education. In reality, I most likely should have taken a year off from school to determine what I wanted to do with my life.

History is a great teacher if you learn from it.

I almost failed out of college after my freshman year. Sound familiar? Doubts resurfaced. *Absolutely nothing has changed. I'm still the same old, lazy, worthless loser everyone thought I was.* I could just imagine my classmates and former teachers shaking their heads, knowing this would be my ultimate outcome. What a waste of energy and time spent worrying about what other people thought!

Where was my head? It was completely inward focused. I was struggling with self-consciousness and doubt about my ability to succeed in anything, let alone at the university level.

I went home that summer and announced to my father that I was going to drop out of college and go into the military. Sensing that I might be prone to impulsive and irrational choices, he **strongly** encouraged me to re-consider and go back for my sophomore year and give it another try. I somehow scraped my act together and finally started going to classes.

About the same time, a young student by the name of Chad Hurley was also attending Indiana University of Pennsylvania (IUP). He ran track and had an interest in computer technology and the arts.

He graduated in 1999 with his B.A. Fine Arts and got a job with a young start-up called PayPal. Chad was responsible for designing the blue PayPal logo. After PayPal, Chad and a couple of co-workers began another venture start-up called YouTube.

Talk about two divergent paths. We both finished high school in 1995. We both began IUP that summer 1995. We both had an aptitude for computers and the arts. Chad went on to become the CEO of one of the most significant web content sharing sites today and one of the youngest multi-millionaires at the time his company sold to Google for $1.65B. Whereas I was barely passing my courses, had just met my advisor for the first time in two years, and was still considering joining the military for job security and health benefits.

Chad and I had the same access to the computer labs, professors, and student activities. We took the same classes, stayed in identical dorms and had the same meal plan.

So what was the difference? He had big dreams. Chad had grand visions of building a global e-commerce site whereas I wanted to get through my "American Studies and Culture" class with a D-.

Don't Limit Your Dreams

Chasing one rabbit doesn't mean you don't dream big, it means you break down big dreams into smaller doable ones. Chad knew he wanted to build a start-up where people could use video to support their businesses, but he had no idea it would take off the way it did. But he listened to his customers and built YouTube one step at a time. In an interview with CNN, Chad stated:

"As you start building the product, don't assume that you know all the answers. Listen to the community and adapt. We had a lot of our own ideas about how the service would evolve. Coming from PayPal and eBay, we saw YouTube as a powerful way to add video to auctions, but we didn't see anyone using our product that way, so we didn't add features to support it." [1]

He didn't know he was going to build one of the biggest Internet sites in the world, but he was always improving and looking for small ways to make the site even better.

Don't limit your dreams.

> **"I have not failed. I've just found 10,000 ways that won't work."**
>
> **~Thomas Edison**

No Big Deal

Are you still worried about failing? Here's an encouragement: you have not arrived yet. Don't fool yourself into thinking that people care that much about your failures. Nobody does, but that's the best thing about chasing your dreams. You don't have time to worry about anyone else.

Focus on what lies just beyond the horizon. Why? You have to move forward to get a better view. *You can't see the next goal until make a move.* Even if it's a small step forward, this creates powerful momentum and a drive to continue.

It's up to you to finish what you started.

Stay the Course

Don't give up too soon. One of the most key ingredients to moving on from failure to success is grit. Remind yourself this is a long distance journey and have the perseverance to stick it out.

How I Became a College Professor

After graduating from college with a grandiose 2.2 GPA, by some serendipitous chain of events, I was hired as a junior-level Information Systems Auditor for a regional accounting and consulting firm. After I had been there for two years, my boss finally told me during an office Christmas party, that he was *'this close'* to not hiring me. "Do you want to know why I chose you over the other candidates?" he asked.

"Sure," I said, *I was immediately curious.* I was waiting for some lightning bolt of insight and wisdom.

"It's because you wore a belt."

I know I shouldn't have taken offense to this. My boss was a little drunk, and a part of me felt really lucky. *After all, imagine how the other guy would feel if he knew?* I couldn't believe such an important life decision was based on an arbitrary fashion choice. Something about that exchange with my boss left an impression. Little things do matter. You will never regret paying attention to detail. Also from that point on, I always wore a belt. Even to bed.

It was a good job, but I didn't quite thrive there. I knew that I didn't want to be an auditor for the rest of my life, so I decided to switch companies. I went to work for one of my client banks for a couple of years, and then in order to move up the corporate ladder, I switched banks a few more times. The only way to move up in the banking world is to become a star commercial lender or move from bank to bank. I finally attained a position of Vice President of Information Security at a mid-sized financial institution.

By all accounts, it was a dream job. It was what I had been reaching for since graduating, and yet something still gnawed at me. I wasn't supposed to be here. I was meant to do something else. Do you ever feel like that?

In 2002 I decided to pursue my dream of going back to graduate school to become a college professor. I went back to school while working full-time to get my graduate degree and completed my doctorate in 2010.

I picked a lane and went for it.

I am now a full-time college professor at Walsh University located in northeast Ohio. Was this where I thought I would be five years ago? Absolutely not. But I love it. Every day is a new day filled with challenges and opportunities. I've had easier jobs, but none more rewarding. I probably spend more time at the 'office' now than I ever did with my corporate job, but this job is completely different. I feel like I am able to affect and change lives for the better. I have found a career that lends itself well to my passion, strengths, and interests.

Will there be another lane in 5 more years? Yes, I'm working on increasing my consulting, writing, and speaking careers. I'm really pleased and satisfied with where I am right now, but I want to continue to grow and challenge myself to new heights.

Don't settle for being okay.

Continue to set new goals once you've met the old ones.

Like a master gardener, you have to prune the rose bush down to its most beautiful parts. Jim Collins in his book *Good to Great* says the greatest enemy to great is good. Cut the good stuff to get to the great stuff.

Pursue what makes you great.

"We are at our very best, and we are happiest, when we are fully engaged in work we enjoy on the journey toward the goal we've established for ourselves. It gives meaning to our time off and comfort to our sleep. It makes everything else in life so wonderful, so worthwhile."

~ Earl Nightingale

Time for You to Start Chasing

You've done the hard work of establishing your goals. You have identified your long and short-term goals based on your strengths, passions, and interests. If you have taken further steps to ensure your success you probably have an A-Team (Accountability Team) to back you up and encourage you along the way. You have established big dreams, visual timelines, and determined what small steps you need to take to get there.

You will falter and make mistakes, and that's okay. An important part of the success journey is overcoming and learning to adjust to your failures. But it's totally worth the effort.

The final step is really the first step.

Start chasing that rabbit.

Conclusion Notes:

1. Chad Hurley. (2006). Interview with CNN Money. http://money.cnn.com/popups/2006/biz2/howtosucceed /6.html.

Philip Kim Biography:

Dr. Philip Kim is an educator, speaker and consultant. Phil has been published in over 20 academic journals and has been invited to present his research at both national and international conferences. As a speaker and consultant he has worked with over 50 small to mid-sized institutions including higher education, financial services, and non-profit organizations.

Phil's first book, *Big Business Problems: Small Business Solutions* (2012) has been well-received and reviewed on Amazon. Phil was also one of the recipients of the Best Paper Award (recognized as the top 5%) at the Conference for Applied Information Systems (CONISAR) 2012 held in New Orleans, LA.

Before becoming a business professor at Walsh University, Phil served as the Vice President of Information Security for a $5B financial services organization, where he was responsible for managing the bank's information security environment and engineered the bank's internal IT risk management practices.

Raised by first generation Korean immigrants, Phil has worked at all of his parents businesses including 7-11 convenience stores, gas stations, diners, and restaurants. He understands the value of hard work and education. His passion is to use his knowledge and expertise to help others achieve their life's goals.

You can visit Phil at his blog at www.write15minutes.com and his consulting site at www.ideapathconsulting.com.

Other Books:

Look inside ↓

Big Business Problems: Small Business Solutions is about addressing the common, daily, recurring problems within most organizations, like managing your employees, customers, vendors, and your technology.

This book will ask and answer the questions you need for your business to thrive in the information age. Questions like: How can I use Mobile Apps to increase productivity? What is SEO and should it matter to me? Should I go to the Cloud? Will it really save me money and time?

Regardless of size, sector, or industry, you will encounter business problems that disguise themselves as "technology" issues. Well, do you consider yourself a tech-expert? Most managers do not. This book is a reference guide for small business owners, managers, and the ones responsible for managing their own technology environment.

You can read this book from beginning to end or as 11 separate topics. Pick and choose the chapters that matter most to you, and especially take advantage of the Top 10 Take-a-ways at the end of each chapter.

This book, co-written by Dr. Philip Kim and 11 contributing authors bring a vast array of expertise in consulting, auditing, banking, education, healthcare, and technology. Their unique insights, tips, and perspectives make this book a must-have in your small business toolbox.

Purchase now at Amazon for only $4.99: http://www.amazon.com/Big-Business-Problems-Small-Solutions-ebook/dp/B008F8H29G

33532669R00094

Made in the USA
Charleston, SC
16 September 2014